MUHAMMAD ALI

MUHAMMAD ALI

A View From the Corner

by Ferdie Pacheco, M.D.
The Fight Doctor

A BIRCH LANE PRESS BOOK
Published by Carol Publishing Group

A Birch Lane Press Book
Published by Carol Publishing Group
Birch Lane Press is a registered trademark of Carol Communications, Inc.
Editorial Offices: 600 Madison Avenue, New York, N.Y. 10022
Sales & Distribution Offices: 120 Enterprise Avenue, Secaucus, N.J. 07094
In Canada: Canadian Manda Group, P.O. Box 920, Station U,
    Toronto, Ontario M8Z 5P9

Queries regarding rights and permission should be addressed to Carol
Publishing Group, 600 Madison Avenue, New York, N.Y. 10022

Carol Publishing Group books are available at special discounts for bulk
purchases, for sales promotions, fund raising, or education purposes.
Special editions can be created to specifications. For details, contact:
Special Sales Department, Carol Publishing Group, 120 Enterprise Avenue,
Secaucus, N.J. 07094

Manufactured in the United States of America
10 9 8 7 6 5 4 3 2 1

Library of Congress Cataloging-in-Publication Data

Pacheco, Ferdie.
    Muhammad Ali : a view from the corner / by Ferdie Pacheco.
        p.   cm.
    ISBN 1-55972-100-6
    1. Ali, Muhammad, 1941-   . 2. Boxers (Sports)—United States—
Biography. I. Title.
    GV1132.A44P33   1992
796.8'3'092—dc20
[B]   92-1260
                                                                CIP

To Chris Dundee
who allowed me into his upside down, crazy,
unusual world of boxing. The basics I
learned from Chris in the Fifth Street Gym,
the refinements of the game from watching
him in action throughout the world.

Contents

Book Three: The Ali Circus and Its Aftermath

Acknowledgments

The book is a small reflection of what life in boxing is like, as seen from the corner, from the gym, from the smoker fights to the glamour fights. None of this could have existed without the fighters, from four-round pugs, to opponents, to contenders, to champions to superstar champions. So, first in line, I bow my head in thanks to the men who put everything on the line when they walk into the squared circle.

To the little gray men of gyms from tank towns to Miami to Vegas to the Big Apple: Ray Arcel, the professor of them all, Angelo Dundee, the best now in action, Gil Clancy, Freddie Brown, Chicky Ferrara, Lou Duva, Georgie Benton, Ace Marotta, Eddie 'The Clot' Aliano, Emmanual Stewart, Eddie Futch, and the many tough men who teach boxers, then support, heal, and motivate them to give their best.

Promoters are a different breed, but without them boxing would not survive, so I tip my hat to Teddy Brennan, to Aileen Eaton and her crafty partner George Parnassus, to Chris Dundee, Don King, Dan Duva, Bob Arum, Don Chargin, Murad Muhammad, Jarvis Astaire, Mickey Duff, and many men who tried to be promoters only to find that it is a highly competitive business and the waters are controlled by denizens of the deep.

To many boxers I worked with, most of whom were managed by Angelo Dundee. To the champions: Luis Manuel Rodriguez, Sugar Ramos, Ultiminio "Sugar" Ramos, Jimmy Ellis, Willy Pastrano, Sugar Ray Robinson (one fight), Hands o' Stone Roberto Duran, Vincente Rondon, Robinson Garcia, Jose Legra, Emile Griffith (one fight), and the greatest champion of all time, Muhammad Ali.

To the cynical, know-it-all armies of the deadline, the boxing writers. The old guys, tough but sentimental, who had seen it all and invented some: Jimmy Cannon, Al Buck, Jesse Abramson, Gentleman Harold Conrad, Red Smith, Jim Murray, Jack Fiske, A. J. Leibling, Bob Waters, and their ilk. To the new guys who rode the Ali Circus: Jerry Lisker, Ed Pope, Jerry Esinberg, Dave Anderson, Fausto Miranda, Pat Putnum, Ed Skylar, and Wally Mathews. And to the men who write about boxing from the heart, Budd Schulberg, Norman Mailer, Gary Smith, and Tom Hauser.

To the jolly men from overseas, who arrive bleary eyed from their transatlantic flight and endeavor to remain that way until they leave. To Peter Wilson, Colin Hart, Peter Moss, Ken Jones, Frankie Taylor, Reggie Gutteridge, and the boxing writer with the finest command of the English language, Hugh McIlvaney.

And finally, to my wife Luisita, whose solving of the mysteries of the word processor led to finishing the text in record time. Like all of us who rode on the Ali Circus, and paid a price, she paid: she typed the manuscript.

BOOK ONE

Ali the Legend, Ali the Man

Chapter 1

The Man Behind the Legend

Many tumultuous years have passed since a tall, handsome boxer named Cassius Clay came into my Miami clinic in 1960 and caused a virtual riot in the office, and I have had a long time to observe the phenomenon that he became. No one, including himself, has been able to get a handle on the many-sided meteor the world eventually knew as Muhammad Ali.

The teenage giant Cassius Clay hit the door talking, and did not stop until he departed, leaving the rest of my patients—indigent blacks, young, old, infirm, beautiful, or ugly—to agree with my nurse's conclusion:

"That chile is going to be sumtin'."

In the early sixties I ran a charity clinic in the Overtown ghetto in Miami. Those years were years of segregation, and the blacks had settled into the bustling community known as Overtown, or in tougher areas known as the Swamp.

In this environment the flower that was the young Cassius Clay

3

The champ standing in front of the author's vintage Packard. *Photo courtesy Luisita Pacheco*

bloomed and flourished. Here, he was safe from the dangers of mixing with white folks, whom he viewed with guarded suspicion, an attitude drilled into him by his racist father. The young man loved his community and felt at home to wander its streets, shucking and jiving with his black brothers, shadowboxing, sparring with anyone who wanted to try to hit an elusive target, and charming the ladies with his good looks and wit.

And the ghetto loved him back. Through the innocence of his white trainer, Angelo Dundee, Cassius was placed in the Mary Elizabeth Hotel, which was to the world of the corrupt what St. Peter's represents to Catholics. The rooms were filled with whores, johns, pimps, boosters, grifters, con men, and addicts.

Cassius Clay at nineteen, in 1960, was unworldly. Nothing in his upbringing had prepared him for this.

He attracted women like a magnet, but he seemed oblivious to them. Oh, he liked them all right, but he was on a quest, he had a mission: He was going to be the Heavyweight Champion of the Whole Wide World! Boxers lived monastic lives in those days, trained by monklike, celibate old men who preached the doctrine of abstinence. "Sex got more fighters knocked out than any left hook ever did," said the wizened old men. Nat Fleischer, publisher and editor of *Ring* magazine, wrote a manual, "How to Train Boxers," and he started his chapter on sex with the dictum: "Masturbation is the scourge of Western Civilization." (I suppose it's acceptable in the East, since they don't have much boxing.)

Cassius Clay had won a gold medal in the 1960 Olympic Games in Rome, where he had been given a dollop of publicity and tasted the heady wine of celebrityhood. He liked both. He intuitively understood stardom, and he felt that it was inevitable that he would be a star, a champion, a millionaire, and have the world at his feet. He not only *felt* it—he *knew* it.

So the people in the ghetto adopted him. He was their giant toy, their baby. Pimps trying to fix him up with foxy ladies would be taken aside and told to lay off "the Champ."

"Boy's going to be a champ," his protectors would say.

"Man's got to have pussy," the pimp would grouse as he pulled away his whore.

Ali jives in Miami's Overtown ghetto, brightening the harsh realities of life. *Photo courtesy Luisita Pacheco*

"Man mus' be a sissy," the rejected hussy would hiss as she was led away.

Yes, that thought persisted throughout his stay in Miami. It excited the few sissies, but they soon came down to earth after trying him a few times.

Finally, *everyone* in the ghetto got the message:

"Protect this kid. He's going to be the Heavyweight Champion of the Whole Wide World!"

But we're getting ahead of our story. Where did he come from? What were his origins? And how did such a peaceful, fun-loving, kind, gentle, loving man come to the rude, brutal, hurtful sport of boxing?

Punching the bag. *Photo courtesy Hy Simon*

Chapter 2

The Clay Family

The family of Cassius Clay, Sr., and Odessa Grady Clay was distinctly middle-class. They lived in a nice house in Louisville, Kentucky; the children, Cassius and Rudy, dressed well and went to a good school. The problems of the ghetto were alien to them. No abandonment by the father, no abuse, no violence, no gangs, no switchblades or zip guns. Cassius Clay grew up in loving surroundings, with the gentle, sweet Odessa as his role model, and his father, the fiery, artistic Cassius Senior, as his motivator.

What did the young Cassius learn from them?

Odessa was a light-skinned, beautiful woman who was soft-spoken, kind, gentle, and religious. She had the good qualities of a devout Christian hómemaker and no obvious bad qualities. She was a peacemaker, a soother, a compromiser. When Cassius Senior was in his cups and came home snorting fire, railing at the injustices of the white world that wouldn't recognize his talents, that held him back from financial gain, that treated him "like a nigger" no matter how evident his superiority was, Odessa would pacify him. And if, on occasion, he took a swing at her, she would not flinch. If he took a swing at a wide-eyed Cassius Junior, she would

8

stand between them, sheltering her son, taking the blow. Wife-beating was a fact of Southern black life, and no unusual notice was given to a black eye or a fat lip on a Sunday morning at church. Not that this was standard conduct at the Clay house, for it wasn't, but it did happen often enough for Clay to later remark to me in his usual sly, funny way:

"Maybe that's when I learned to float like a butterfly. . . . I owe my defense to my father."

Perhaps, but what he also learned from his father was a deep distrust of the white man.

Cassius Clay, Sr., was a handsome man with talents in singing and painting. Louisville was a small town in which these talents could not grow. He would never be recognized in Louisville, never be given his due. Oh, he made good money painting signs, but it was hardly the acceptance for which he longed. Frustrated by the tough segregation laws of the South and unwilling to move his family north, he lived a life of anguished depression. If only the white man did not exist to push him back, to stifle his creative urges, Cassius Clay, Sr., could be recognized for what he was: an artist.

The young Clay, his head filled with his father's racist dogma, was never fully comfortable around whites. Somewhere along his long road in boxing he would learn that not *all* whites were bad, and that not *all* blacks were good, but that maturity took a long time coming, and even today no one in his inner circle is white. Oh, he has white friends whom he likes, and is warmly friendly with Angelo and Chris Dundee, Gene Kilroy, and assorted show business friends, but the fact is that although the white man considers himself a great friend of Ali's, Ali does not reciprocate.

It has always been part of Ali's success with people to make them *think* that he is listening to every word they say, that he will do exactly as they suggest, that they are extremely important to him, that he is grateful that they are interested in helping him. He even gives a great show of following their advice . . . then does what *he* wants. A perfect example of this occurred when Dick Gregory came to him with a great plan for nutrition and weight reduction. Ali, always willing to try a new way to work off the pounds added by his huge ingestion of cakes, pies, and ice cream, eagerly acquiesced. Gregory then set up a system of high-colonic irrigations, much to Ali's horror. After a course of these irrigations, which Ali later described with the humor of a man who had endured the torture of the Inquisition, Gregory put Ali on a diet of rhizomes, roots, granules, and pills that had one common property—they were all *tasteless*.

How did Ali react? Ali ate these tasteless, nutritious foods, drank chalky, muddy shakes, and smiled a great deal at Gregory. Then, with the Nutrition Guru safely out of sight, Ali called for Lana Shabazz, his wondrous cook, and she prepared a full "down home" meal, which Ali devoured.

In San Diego, before the first Norton fight, Ali suffered a slight ankle sprain. One of his entourage had been in the National Football League and knew the Chargers' trainer, so right before the fight, in the dressing room, Ali had his ankle wrapped. The only problem was that Ali was not a fullback, a lineman, or a quarterback. He needed mobility, needed to be loose and agile, so he could float like a butterfly.

No sooner had Ali finished telling his NFL friend how grateful he was for his help, how he owed his well-being to him, how he couldn't have fought without him, than he signaled for the scissors. Off came the tight, professionally wrapped ankle tapes. Once again Ali had been too polite and courteous to say no; once again Ali had sacrificed his comfort to make someone feel good; once again Ali had done what *he* wanted.

His relationship with his younger brother Rudy (now Rahaman) bears observation. The older Cassius was protective of Rudy from the time they were children; Cassius was light-skinned and possessed an almost feminine beauty, qualities inherited from Odessa; Rudy was dark and handsome, very masculine, like his father.

As Cassius Clay rose in the world of boxing, Rudy tagged along, trying desperately to be as good in the ring as his big brother. But alas, when the boxing genes had been distributed, Ali had gotten them all. Poor Rudy tried to compete, but was ill equipped.

As Cassius grew famous, a strange drama unfolded in the gym. Cassius recognized that Rudy had inherited some of his father's stubbornness and sense of outrage. The more Cassius tried to persuade Rudy to quit, the harder Rudy tried. Noted for his easy sparring sessions, Cassius would turn vicious when working with Rudy. Day after day he would administer a fearful beating. Cassius was saying to Rudy, "I love you too much to see you get beaten up in the ring. Man, you ain't got it. You're going to get hurt. Get out. I got enough for us both. You'll never be broke as long as I'm alive."

Rudy was stubborn. He would not quit, and the beatings escalated.

Oh, Rudy attempted to develop a boxing career. Won some, lost some. He was an ordinary fighter, never would be a contender, but he nonetheless tried desperately to keep up with Cassius. How could poor Rudy have known that for two decades, *nobody* would be able to keep up with this meteor?

And Cassius worried. It bothered him. He did not want to see his brother beaten. He did not want to see him hurt. He did not want to hurt him, but what could he do but beat him half to death every day at the Fifth Street Gym?

Finally, Rudy involved himself with a higher discipline, the Black Muslims, who ordered him to stop fighting. Ali breathed a sigh of relief. No more humiliations, no more beatings. Ali made a vow to see that his brother never wanted for material things, a vow he has kept very well, but the old worries returned, and with them, a new one: guilt.

As Rudy reached his late twenties, he began to have head pains and to experience imbalance, and it was widely rumored that Rudy had brain damage from the beatings he had taken in the gym—or, worse, that he had a brain tumor.

Ali is not a man to dwell on his past or to deal in guilt. He lives in the *now*; yesterday is gone and forgotten. Yet such is his love for his brother that he *did* feel responsibility, did feel guilt.

Nothing came of the rumor. There was no brain tumor, and if there was brain damage, Rudy was able to conceal it well, since on his healthiest day he was not a talker. So the two brothers remained close, as they are to this day.

For me this bond is encapsulated by one scene. It's the night of the first Sonny Liston fight, a night filled with high drama. Rumors of assassination attempts on Ali's life are everywhere. The Klan is out to get him for turning Muslim; the Mafia will get him if he beats Liston. The new bodyguards, the Fruit of Islam, surround Ali, protecting him in their tight, black four-button, suits. Ali is being hustled into his dressing room. He is, as usual, doing what he is told. But wait a minute, hold on—Ali breaks away, strides into the arena, and stands in the aisle, intently peering into the ring. In an undercard fight, his brother is taking a beating from a run-of-the-mill boxer. Ali flinches with every blow; he seems to be taking the blows himself; he moves with every punch; he rocks his shoulders. He is fighting Rudy's fight—and, one other thing: He is crying.

"My brother ain't never going to fight again."

From that fight on, I looked at Ali in a different light. He was, and is, a devoted family man. No one—not even the Muslims, who

The brothers Ali.

tried—could get Ali to forsake his family. For this, I commend him. There's a lot more to Ali than meets the eye. I could never have imagined the extent of his uniqueness on that exciting February night in Miami Beach when Ali finally became the Heavyweight Champion of the Whole Wide World!

Chapter 3

Boxing Style

I distinctly remember the first time I went to the Fifth Street Gym to watch Clay work. The gym was filled to capacity with working fighters and their managers and trainers, and the young Cassius Clay was a minor player among stars of the ring wars. Chris Dundee, the promoter of all Miami Beach fights, had been in the fight game since he was old enough to say "We wuz robbed," and his busy venue attracted fighters from all over the country who were looking for work, looking to get taken on by Chris or his industrious trainer-manager brother, Angelo.

The exodus of great Cuban fighters had accelerated under Castro's regime, and so the gym held Cuban champions like Sugar Ramos, Mantequilla Napoles, and Luis Manuel Rodriguez, and top Cuban contenders like Florentino Fernandez, Douglas Vallant, Robinson Garcia, Baby Luis, and many more. Angelo also managed world champions Willie Pastrano and Ralph Dupas, so the place was filled with quality fighters. The old pros were the best, veterans of Gleason's Gym and Jacob's Beach, canny cornermen of a thousand nights in smoke-filled arenas where the fight announcer always ended the introductions with:

14

"And may the better 'ticipant 'merge trumpet!"

So here they stand at the edge of the ring apron, stubby arms folded over potbellies, thick cigars clamped between yellowing teeth, rheumy eyes squinting. The Gray Men watch the agile Willy Pastrano pop his painless jab, then nod in appreciation.

"Some jab," says Sellout Moe.

"Uses it like a paintbrush," says Chicky.

And then the welterweight Luis Manuel Rodriguez comes into the ring, and they all smile. Luis is working out with middleweight Florentine Fernandez. Odds are if he hits Luis one good hook, Luis will land back in Havana.

"Give you better odds," says Golub. "If he *ever* hits Luis with a hook, I'll buy you a new cigar."

Effortlessly, Luis glides clockwise around the ring, Floro in pursuit, throwing his nuclear hooks and hitting only the ring ropes. Now, Luis shifts gears and goes the other way, all the while jumping up and down in front of Floro, popping his forehead with a mosquitolike jab that takes Floro's mind off homicide.

Standing behind the College of Pugilistic Cardinals is a tall, good-looking boxer, dressed in clean gym clothes, gloved up, waiting to go on. The boy has observed every move Pastrano and Rodriguez have made. He is a sponge. He is here to learn, to add to what he knows, to develop his talent, to take advantage of his great ability and God-given body.

"Clay's up next," says Sully, shifting a dead cigar stub in his toothless mouth. "Get up dere, ya mud toitle," he says without a hint of a smile.

Clay is in with a journeyman boxer named Willy Johnson, who knows the ropes inside out and has sparred with champions. The bell rings and Clay touches gloves with Johnson, bringing a snort from the Gray Men.

"Amateur stuff," harrumphs Chappy.

"He better forget he win a gold medal," says Evil Eye. "He does dat in Joisey, he gets a mouthful of leather."

Clay is circling now, imitating Luis and popping a painless jab like Pastrano. The kid learns fast.

"Take a dip," says Angelo, eyes glued to the new kid, a big smile on his face. "Slide over. Pop the right." Clay responds; it all works. "Ain't he sumptin'," says Angelo, barely able to restrain his joy.

"Yeah, he's sumptin', all right, but if he holds his hands down like that he's gonna get fuckin' killed."

"What's he leaning back from a punch for? Didn't you teach him better'n that, Angie? Liston would catch him on the end of that pull-back and fuckin' kill the kid."

"He can't fuckin' punch," says Lou Gross. "The kid's a shoe-maker. A heavyweight without a punch gets fuckin' killed."

"Headhunter. The kid don't t'row to the body. No body shots, no head shots to follow—without a body attack the kid ain't going nowheres. In the big time the kid gets fuckin' killed."

"Kill the body, and the head is sure to follow," they all say in unison, puffing furiously on their cigars.

Well, Ali's fighting days are over now, and an intensive study of his style would reveal that the College of Pugilistic Cardinals had been right in their observations of the young Cassius Clay, but wrong in their conclusions.

Ali turned his faults into advantages. His great hand speed made it possible to hold his left at his waist. His leg speed made it possible to lean back, away from a punch. To hit Ali when he leaned back, you needed a stepladder and blinding speed. Ali gave you the body, and while you busily worked it, he pounded your head. (See the Frazier fights; study the Foreman bout.) And he had the leg speed of a welterweight. And hand speed. And radar for incoming punches. And a granite chin. And one of the greatest boxing brains ever seen in a prize ring. What else can one ask of a fighter? One thing: a mouth. Nonstop talking, bell to bell, to frustrate you, to wear you out, to confuse, befuddle, distract.

He was a master of fight psychology. He knew what to say. He used it like a weapon. It had never been seen before, and it has not been used effectively since.

Cagey men have dissected his style. One of ringdom's great professors is the scholarly Eddie Futch, who worked with two fighters who beat Ali—Ken Norton and Joe Frazier. Here is his keen analysis of Ali:

1. He held his hands too low.

2. He pulled back from a punch.
3. He always moved clockwise.

Futch, a master of the game, balanced out his critique with one sentence that made the above meaningless: "He had so much ability, he could always outrun his mistakes."

Ali's boxing life was divided into six phases:

A. *Amateur Champion.* Gold medal, 1960, Rome. As a light heavyweight, he was so fast that he dazzled his opponents, the judges, and the fans. Hand speed was a big plus factor here.

B. *Contender.* From October 1960 to February 1964, Ali polished his boxing style, learned from his idols Sugar Ray Robinson and Jack Johnson, and perfected his style with Willy Pastrano and Luis Rodriguez. It was here that he also found and developed his "Act," which continued until he won the title.

C. *First Championship: 1968.* These years saw the bubbly, fun-loving Ali turn sullen and ugly as he pursued vendettas against Floyd Patterson and Ernie Terrell. For the fans this was the peak of his "float like a butterfly, sting like a bee" style. Ali was at his fastest here. He did not believe in allowing his opponent to land one good, solid shot. He was a blur in the ring. The Cleveland Williams fight saw Ali at his fastest and sharpest. Toward the end of this reign he expressed boredom, moaned about retirement, and was unhappy because he had no real opponent to excite him.

D. *The Exile and Second Coming of Ali: 1974.* By 1973, Ali had been in exile for three years. He had refused to be inducted into the Army, had taken a stand against the Vietnam War, had said he was a conscientious objector. The government indicted him and yanked his passport, and boxing turned its back on him.

When he finally returned he found he had lost some of his skills. The great leg speed was gone. He was still fast, but in spurts. Now, he needed to pace himself, to look for rests, to use guile instead of speed. Without speed, it was apparent that he would have to take punishment. Could he do that? Was he tough enough to withstand heavyweight punishment? The answer to these questions would soon come, in his tune-up fights against Jerry Quarry in Atlanta and Oscar Bonavena in New York.

The answer was good and bad. The good was that he could take a punch; the bad was the same. For his immediate future, finding out he could withstand the heaviest shot was an immense relief. We all knew he had the inner toughness to survive, but no one can measure the "toughness" of the brain to receive a heavy blow. Ali passed all tests with flying colors. From now to the end of his career he would dance a bit, rest a bit, and, if he had to take punishment, take a bit—or more.

On the other hand, this did not bode well for his future health. Repetitive, hard blows to the head over a long period of years are not considered to be of therapeutic value. Heavyweight pounding over a long period of time will cause midbrain damage, a fact Ali was not willing to understand. All he or anyone else cared about was "now," not tomorrow. "Now," Ali was back, he was once again the Heavyweight Champion of the Whole Wide World.

E. *The Final Phase.* From 1977 to 1980 the Legend wound down. Ali's championship sailed the seas on a wild, worldwide ride, and he gained international fame unparalleled in the history of sports. At this time he was without question one of the most recognizable faces in the world. He paid the price in wear and tear. His health began to show the effects of the beatings; his domestic life disintegrated into a serial-monogamy festival. The Ali Circus rumbled on, until at last he came to what seemed like the last farce, a Las Vegas fight on February 15, 1978, with a 7-0-1 heavyweight named Leon Spinks.

Ali, undertrained and overconfident, lost his title to an inexperienced, blown-up cruiserweight. It appeared to be an ignominious end to a brilliant career.

F. *The Resurrection and the Light That (Finally) Failed.* Ali prepared for one last face-saving foray into ring immortality. He would win back his title for an unprecedented third time. Once again he would shock and amaze his critics, once again he'd be carried aloft by the aging members of the Ali Circus into a humid New Orleans night, once again he would hear the crowd roar, "Ali! Ali! Ali!"

That accomplished, Ali did not go away quietly. The forces that profited from his desire to stay at center stage had more battles lined up. Health considerations were swept under the ring rug.

Once more Ali was called out to battle a new, strong, young champion, Larry Holmes.

"He was my sparring partner! I'll whup him like I was his daddy! I'm back. I'll shock and amaze you!"

Ali screamed his doggerel and the faithful listened and believed. Had he ever let them down? Had he not shocked and amazed them? Had he not always painted himself into a corner and fought his way out?

"He's not of this earth; my guy is from outer space. He ain't human. He will win," said Angelo Dundee, whose love and faith in Ali was so great it blinded his judgment.

His sparring was awful. His sparring partners held back, afraid to "hurt" him. He had *never* looked good in the gym, they said.

Ali, determined to come in at around 212 pounds, his best weight, permitted a doctor to give him thyroid hormone, amphetamines, and diuretics.

Ali was now not only in danger of losing the fight, but of losing his life.

One has to thank the generous Larry Holmes, who, loving Ali, held back, trying not to hurt his idol. Nonetheless, for us—we who had seen the bright-faced teenager with the flying feet and the big mouth, we who had traveled the globe with the Ali Circus—the fight was as tragic an event as seeing the legendary Joe Louis sprawled on the ring apron at Madison Square Garden, knocked out by a savage Rocky Marciano.

There remained a farce in the Bahamas with Trevor Berbick, but that was only a sad postscript to the Holmes debacle.

Chapter 4

Ali and the Ladies

Until he was almost out of his teens, Ali was so absorbed in his Spartan training regime that he did not pay much attention to the fairer sex. Not that he didn't look, or even perhaps want to touch, but any distraction from training was rigidly avoided.

When he launched into his professional tour, Ali became the hunted rather than the hunter. A beautiful specimen of manhood, with his sculpted body, smooth skin, and angelic face, he stood out in the crowd. Add to these physical qualities a sparkling, fun-loving personality, publicity and media attention, and a spectacular boxing career, and one can appreciate the sexual magnet that he became. It is a great wonder, given the prodigious womanizer that he became, that he did not succumb to feminine blandishments earlier than he did. In part it was due to his inexperience, in part to his determination to arrive at his goal, and in part to the absence in his life of experienced, hard-living, wenching cornermen. In the beginning the entourage was small, mainly the worldly innocent, happily married Angelo Dundee; the mute Luis Sarria, a serious Cuban masseur; and a few cornermen who came and went, such as Solomon McAteer.

Ali headquartered in Miami to be close to Angelo and the Fifth Street Gym. By the time of the first Liston fight in 1964, Ali had bought a modest home in the north section, parked his bus outside, and started entertaining in a serious way. Girls were never a problem for Ali. They lined up to see him, touch him, talk to him. Music stars such as Gladys Knight, Diana Ross, and others joined the growing army of admirers, and Ali, the great humanist, treated them all the same. Ali had an old-world courtliness, a sympathetic, admiring, complimentary way about him when he was around the ladies. He was a true democrat. He treated each one, young or old, rich or poor, beautiful or ugly, famous or unknown, the same way: royally.

If given a hard time by a tough woman, or if his puritanical sensibility was offended, Ali could turn as cold as a polar blast. He would ice up and move on. He did not, possibly could not, resort to physical violence.

In examining his life from the present back to his childhood in Louisville, one can appreciate how he formulated this courtly attitude toward women. Quite simply, he was his mother's child. Odessa was kind, quiet, soothing to be with, eager to please, and the kind of woman Ali sought to marry all his life. It does not take a Freudian analyst to understand the deep imprint that the sweet Odessa, a perfect mother, a near-perfect woman, had on the impressionable Ali. It was to his credit that he found at least two other Odessas in his life, and to his discredit that he lost one.

In New York City for the Doug Jones fight in 1963, Ali met and hired a man who was to have a deep influence on his life. Drew Bundini Brown was a consummate street artist. He was the François Villon of Harlem: street-smart and tough on one side, sweet, sensitive, and loving on the other. With a lot of hard living and loving behind him, Bundini met Ali at just the right time. Ali needed a Sancho Panza, a man who could teach him about life — not the sweet life of Louisville and Odessa, but the hard life of Harlem and Mack the Knife. More on Bundini later, but what he brought to Ali was an awareness of the world of the "Lush Life," of Ellington, of "Sophisticated Ladies," of the sweet rewards of the bedroom. Never has a professor had a more attentive student.

By the time of the Liston buildup and fight, Ali had fallen in love. Fallen for the first girl that fit the mold. She was cute. She was funny. She was talented. She was half in the world of show business, half in the demimonde.

She was also honed in on Ali. She ate up every word he said; laughed, cried, rooted, cheered, exhorted in his victories. Never had a knight a more loyal lady than Sonji Roi. They were lovebirds, and even the Gray Men of the gym had to bite hard on their cigars lest they criticize her to Ali.

Like many young men poleaxed by the hot searing blast of love, irretrievably enmeshed in the clutches of lust, Ali rushed pell-mell into marriage. It seemed the only way to have her, possess her, not risk losing her.

Sonji Roi was a very likable person, and projected a wholesome image, in keeping with Ali's puritanical views on womanhood. The fact was that no one outside of Sonji's sister was thrilled with this marriage. The future King of Boxing had married beneath himself.

Ali's family was less than happy, and his boxing family was down-right glum. The consensus was that Sonji had lured Ali to the altar on the strength of her expertise in the ways of the bedroom. Rumor had it that Sonji was an artist who could demonstrate the *Kamasutra* in all its rich splendors. Sex was not a subject with which gym rats were very conversant, or very enlightened.

It was during the long buildup for the Liston title fight in Miami that Ali's life took another, more serious turn. The Miami Overtown ghetto was a beehive of Black Muslim recruiting activity, and Ali was a prime candidate. Eventually recruited by his brother Rudy, Ali joined the Muslims, and they changed his views on matrimony.

This was the first step in the Sonji-Ali marital breakup. As is true of most young marriages forged in the fire of pelvic discovery, this one could not stand harsh reality, in this case the puritanical fire of the Muslim belief. Ali fell totally under the spell of Malcolm X, and good-time Sonji took a distinct second place in Ali's life. It was not a position she was used to, comfortable in, or would tolerate long.

Sonji made a stab at turning Muslim, trying to please the now-fanatical Ali, but her heart and body were not in it. She had struggled too hard to get to where she was to fall back to the rear of the crowd, shrouded in linens, sans makeup, sans jewelry, sans furs, sans glamour.

"No, no, baby," her voice kept saying, "you don't have to take this shit from *nobody*! You are Ali's wife. They got to *show* you, baby, you got to be up there in front, lookin' fine, being your foxy, hot self."

It did not take long to show Sonji the door, pay her a million, and say good-bye. Sassy Sonji was gone with a minimum of fuss. Ali mooned and looked sad for a while, but with the Muslims preaching fire and brimstone in his ear, and with Sportin' Life Bundini telling him there were scads of Sassy Sonjis in every town, and with the black stars of song calling again, and with Angelo laying out another boxing tour, and with Sweet Odessa assuring him that all would be right again in no time, Ali did what he would always do: wake up, look in the mirror, and yell, "I am the heavyweight champion. Ain't I pretty?"

And then the small Ali Circus would mount the bus and start on another magical tour into fistic history.

With serious Muslim commitment came serious pressure to marry a decent, sane, sober Muslim lady. To Ali this seemed a blessing. He was seeking order in his life.

Intuitively, Ali sought surcease from the pelvic chase. It was not good for a boxer to chase, or be chased, by the foxy ladies. The Gray Men would tell him: "It's not the pussy that gets you—it's the *chasing* the pussy. The late hours. The nightlife."

They would quote chapter and verse from the Gleason's Gym manager, who said: "As soon as a black guy straightens out his hair, throw him out of the gym."

Was this a racist remark, or the harsh realities of the gym? What did they mean?

Well, in those days, the fancy men of Harlem were all straightening out their naps and dressing like uptown dudes. Gym rats felt that boxers who behaved in this fashion were into "chasing" and weren't paying attention to business. They were adjudicated as being less than worthless, and were banished.

What was actually written inside the thirties' skull of the Gray Men was more succinctly put in the argot of the time.

"When a nigger straightens out his nap, t'row the bum out."

Chapter and Verse

Ali heard it from a different sound system, but it was just as true, and infinitely more compelling.

Elijah Muhammad was fond of Ali. The head of the Muslim nation found in Ali a man who could validate the religion, make it credible, and recruit large numbers into its ranks. It would not do to have a tomcat like Ali get adverse publicity. The solution was to get him married to a proper Muslim lady. But being a wise man, the Honorable Elijah knew he had to come up with a Muslim queen, a jewel, a beauty equal in attractiveness to Ali. She also had to be as obedient as a Muslim wife, but have a soupçon of fire, of independence, of modified rebellion; Ali did not like doormats. And the Honorable Elijah had to make sure she was highly intelligent, and a true believer; pillow talk had to adhere to the party line.

Well, that was one tall order. Where to find such a woman?

Right under their noses. One of the Muslim leaders ran a bakery, and in it worked a tall, statuesque, natural beauty named Belinda Boyd. She was sweet but strong-willed, fiercely determined to be her own person, and nobody's fool. Belinda had the kind of fresh-scrubbed beauty that novelists call "handsome." She was a natural beauty. Her bone structure was superb, her skin light and flawless, her nose straight, and she had a smile that could light up the entire Great Lakes district. She had a fine sense of humor, and a throaty laugh that was contagious. Under her Muslim-prescribed floor-length, flowing robes, one could sense a strong, well-formed body. One got the sense of being in the presence of one of the world's great women, of one of the world's great beauties.

It did not take the alert Ali long to become enamored of her. He contrasted this Muslim queen to Sonji. Poor Sonji's memory evaporated in a puff. Sonji: beehive hairdo, tons of makeup, mascara, eye shadow, pouty mouth covered with garish red lip gloss. Sonji, with her tight, low-cut dresses and miniskirts, showing her figure to all men. Could you compare her to Belinda, who modestly covered up her beauty, who moved with silent dignity through life, who embraced the Muslim faith with all her heart and soul?

Belinda with her four children. *Photo courtesy AP/Wide World Photos*

Good-bye, Sonji; Hello, Belinda

Life with Belinda was heaven for Ali. She was a childbearing machine. She was a faithful wife. She was a loving wife. She was a partner in life.

When the dog days of the Exile came upon them, Ali wandered the land, restlessly driving from city to city. Belinda understood and kept quiet, never scolding, always understanding. Her man needed an audience. He was a performer, a high-wire act. He needed his stage, and so he went into the night to find an audience, to speak, to roam restlessly in search of excitement. And Belinda waited.

Finally, the harsh Exile was over. Ali was once again on every front page. After Ali-Frazier I, "The Fight," the world beat a path to their door. Belinda understood. Her man was doing what he was meant to do, to be. . . .

Now there flowed money by the truckloads. Now Ali could buy a sumptuous house in Cherry Hill, New Jersey. Now she and her children could have whatever they wanted. But what the money could not purchase, what they wanted, was Ali at home. What they wanted was Ali's time and attention and love. What they got was money and plane schedules, as Ali led his growing Circus to foreign countries to show his fans that he was indeed a world champion. Belinda joined him at times, but she was screened off, left to tend the tent, and it is hard to remember her at these fights.

Now it was time for the Ali Circus to travel to Zaire, Africa, for Ali to reclaim his title from George Foreman in an unusual Black Awakening. For the first time a Black Champion (Foreman) would fight a Black Contender (Ali), promoted by a black man (Don King) in an emerging black African nation, Zaire. The only element missing from this scenario was a black wife: Belinda was left behind.

The long days of training in the African heat were coming to an end when Foreman suffered a cut that would delay the fight for weeks. The heat and weariness were bearable, but the womanless ennui was impossible to take, so Don King, former numbers kingpin of the mean streets of Cleveland, sent off for some quality ladies—cheerleaders, if you will, to liven things up, to get publicity, and to perk up Ali's flagging spirits.

Originally four girls were assigned to each camp, but Ali had great scouts previewing the talent, and soon they spied a tall beauty in the Foreman Camp who seemed to have stepped off a Miss America stage. Ali was at once smitten, and he quickly negotiated a trade.

The African experience was an odd event. Ali arrived expecting to see great black beauty, but his image of black was rooted in his mother's image, in Belinda's beauty, and both those women had a high percentage of white blood in them, as did Ali.

Ali's view of Africans was comical. He could not shake the idea that Africans looked just like American blacks. Over and over he would look at the three promoters, dressed in their woolen Russian trade union suits, and giggle.

"Don't they look just like niggers from Detroit?"

And when Ali had scoured the countryside for a beautiful black girl, he would dejectedly go back to his villa, saying, "These girls are too black; what they need is a little white blood in them."

Racist? Probably, by today's heightened sensibilities, but to Ali he was just speaking his mind. There were no Odessas, Sonjis, no Belindas in Africa. At least there weren't until Veronica Porsche showed up.

Africa proved to be the rocks upon which Ali's matrimonial ship foundered and sank.

Back in America after the Foreman fight, once again the champion, bigger than ever, more sought after than ever, and with a new love interest, Ali sought the refuge of the road. He hit home once in a while, and Belinda traveled with him sometimes, but the only constant in Ali's life was Veronica.

In his original way, Ali played with all manner of possibilities to make three go into one. He announced that Veronica was his assistant. His houseguest. His housekeeper. His baby-sitter. His nursery instructor. Finally, really reaching the outer limits of credibility, he claimed that Veronica was Belinda's cousin—that the two women were friends, shopping together, playing together, and living under the same roof.

It is a tribute to the seriousness with which Muslim women take their marriage vows that Belinda withstood the humiliation as long as she did. Grim-faced, she put up a front, but her heart was

The first Mrs. Ali, Sonji Roi, a beautiful spirit whom the Muslim religion could not tame.

Wife number two, Belinda Boyd, the mother of four of Ali's children. *Photo courtesy AP/Wide World Photos*

The third Mrs. Ali, the beautiful Veronica Porche, at a Lakers basketball game in Los Angeles in September 1979. *Photo courtesy AP/Wide World Photos*

Yolanda Williams at her wedding in Louisville in November 1986. She became the fourth and final (to date) Mrs. Ali.

broken, and she knew she could not, would not, be part of a harem, even a two-woman harem.

The end of the Belinda era came as the Ali Circus traveled to Manila to meet Joe Frazier in what was figured to be an easy fight. Ali actually sought the fight because it gave him a chance to be alone with Veronica for six weeks. It was what the Gray Men call a "Pussy Trip."

The end came when Ali was invited to meet President Ferdinand Marcos and his wife Imelda. Ali made the consummate error of bringing Veronica, and a worse gaffe by introducing her as his wife. Considering that this was seen on international television and written up in all the papers, it was tantamount to flinging the gauntlet in Belinda's face.

President Marcos: "You have a very beautiful wife, Mr. Ali."

Ali: "Yours ain't so bad either."

Enough! Basta!

Belinda jumped on a jet, detoured through Tokyo to get in a little revenge shopping, and steamed into Ali's hotel, dragging twenty-four suitcases behind her. The Ali Circus men shuffled their feet, looked at the floor, and tried to find some other place to be.

The men who lived in camp with Ali had gotten to know and love Belinda. Pat Patterson, the softhearted, tough Chicago cop, tried to say a few words to her, as did cornerman Walter "Blood" Youngblood and Bundini, but Belinda would listen to no one. She had come halfway around the world to get an answer that only Ali could give.

"It's her or me," said Belinda, who soon realized she had lost her man. Back through the lobby went Belinda with the haggard bellhops, loaded with luggage, then on to a return jet and forward into divorce court.

Good-bye, Belinda; Hello, Veronica

Veronica Porsche was a curious blending of Sonji and Belinda. She had Sonji's *au courant* hairstyles, makeup, and modern clothes, and she had Belinda's large, shapely figure, her pure facial beauty, and her soft blend-into-the-background personality. And, like her predecessors, she had more than a dollop of white blood.

During what was left of Ali's boxing life, Veronica formed a part of the traveling menagerie of human flotsam and jetsam known as the Ali Circus. She was quiet, agreeable, circumspect, and did not go out of her way to get to know many of Ali's cronies.

Ali was smitten with her, very protective of her, jealous of the time she spent away from him, and comically puritanical about her being ogled by men.

When Veronica was ready to deliver a child by cesarean section, Ali called me to arrange the operation. Immediately I called a distinguished ob-gyn professor, Ray Simmons, MD, and we booked an operating suite.

Andy Warhol photographs Ali, his wife Veronica, and his infant daughter Hanna, August 1977. *Photo courtesy AP/Wide World Photos*

I found Ali pacing up and down in his suite at the Octagon Towers in Miami Beach. He wore an uncharacteristic nervous look. Veronica looked serene. She was not in pain, and she was waiting patiently for Ali to offer encouragement. Ali was waiting for me. I saw his face and knew he was worried.

"What's the matter? Don't worry about the C-section, it's really easy. We'll be out of there in no time."

I would have invited him in, but I knew how he hated to see blood and operations. Still, his worried look persisted.

"Ali, come on, tell me what's bothering you."

He lowered his huge head, unable to look me in the eye.

"Are you going to be there?" he asked.

"Damned right. No way to assist without being in the room." I couldn't imagine what he was getting at.

"Will you see her naked?"

So that was it. The puritan in Ali was coming out. He did not mind strangers (the doctor, nurses, anesthetist) seeing the beautiful Veronica naked, but it bothered him that a personal friend would see her, even if he were a part of the operating team. I looked at his worried face for a long moment.

"Ali, no one is going to see Veronica naked. Female nurses will prep and drape her before the others come into the room. All we will see is a small patch of skin that looks like any patch of skin from any part of the body."

He looked relieved. I put my arm around one of his broad shoulders.

"Hey, it's a piece of cake. Don't worry about a thing."

We walked out to the limo, and Ali was Ali again, shucking and jiving, having a good time, ready to greet his new offspring.

The downfall of this marriage came when Ali quit boxing and settled in Beverly Hills with Veronica.

If there is a spot on earth that is more relentlessly corrupting than Beverly Hills, I have yet to find it. Morals, principles, and scruples cannot be found. Opportunism, belief in the bottom line, hedonism, and money-mongering can be found aplenty.

It is not a place for the true-of-heart. It is not a place for the naïve. It is not a place for a failing star. It is not a place to seek out for early retirement. In short, it was the worst place Ali could have gone.

Initially, Ali was the toast of Hollywood, and Veronica, with her great beauty, was in big demand. Big stars sought out Ali. Later, they sought out Veronica.

Ali's fame diminished as his injury became more apparent, and the A-list, status-hungry, name-dropping crowd began to pay scant attention to him. He was old news.

Yesterday's star. God knows, Hollywood has status euthanasia developed to a fine art. D. W. Griffith, Keaton, Swanson, Gilbert, Luise Rainer, Von Stroheim, and hundreds of others experienced the humiliation of the Hollywood deep freeze. It is a complete humiliation, well defined. It goes from the boy who parks your car, to the maitre d' who doesn't greet you with an ear-shattering hello, to the waiter who gives you indifferent service at an out-of-the-way table. The Hollywood Humiliation is not nebulous: It is a cold, complete, total shutout. It is an emasculation of surgical proportions.

So Ali, for once in his life, found himself worse than abused; he found himself ignored.

Such was not the case with Veronica, because the sleazes of Beverly Hills like to lurk like wolves at the edge of the campfire, waiting to pounce on easy prey. Veronica, in Movieland, was easy prey.

Ali, infirm but too proud to acknowledge it, ignored by the who's-hot-today subintelligentsia of Beverly Hills, headed for home, mentally, if not physically, leaving the newly discovered Veronica behind.

Good-bye, Veronica; Hello, Lonnie

Ali returned to the Chicago area, where the Muslims are headquartered. He was sick, but not beaten. He was proud and still in great demand, so he picked up the threads of his life and, uncomplaining, went about the life of being a retired champion. He was, after all, the Greatest Heavyweight Champion of All Time . . . of All Time.

Ali had always ridden on Lady Luck's shoulders, so it is not surprising that a little girl who used to sit on his lap when he lived on her street would grow up to be a beautiful, college-educated, Muslim-indoctrinated candidate for Ali's affections. Such is Ali's innate good fortune that this is exactly what happened, and Ali, in his forty-fourth year, with three ex-wives and six children (Maryum, Rasheeda, Jamilla, and Muhammad Jr. by Belinda; and Hana and Laila by third wife Veronica), took his youthful admirer for his fourth wife.

Is this Ali fairy tale unusual? Not if you've ridden with the Ali Circus as long as I have. Hell, it's normal. Ali's luck. There's nothing like it. Just when he's at the end of a limb and is energetically sawing it off, he'll do something to "shock and amaze" you.

I suppose it would be indefensible to write about Ali's ladies and ignore the legions of worshiping females who trooped through his bedroom during the roughly two decades that the Ali Circus rode the globe.

Once I was profiled in *People* magazine and was quoted as saying that Ali was a pelvic missionary. Great was the hue and cry among the lesser members of the Ali Circus. Imagine saying something like that.

"It's true, ain't it?" said Ali with a smile. Remember, Ali was a forgiving sort. I noticed with a cynical smile that the ones yelling the loudest were the advance scouts, the procurers who fed an endless stream of ladies to Ali's suites. What were they mad about? Basically, I had bruised their professional pride. I had said that Ali was bountiful in his pelvic generosity, that he bestowed his favors on the beautiful and the ugly alike. Well, there it was. Professional pride was bashed.

"We never got him no ugly broad," said one of the pelvic outriders.

Let us, for the sake of completeness and now that Ali is happily married and quiescent, put this rather inconsequential aspect of the Ali saga to rest.

Ali was a robust young man who loved women. His giving nature did not leave much room for rejection. Women flocked to him, and he did his best to work them into his schedule.

Ali delighted in stopping his limo at a bus stop where sullen, tired women were standing in the rain, waiting for a ride home.

Ali would bounce out, kissing one and all, especially the fat, the middle-aged, the ugly ones. A hug and a kind word, one for all:

"Um, Mama, you lookin' so fine . . ." A hug. "Wish I had time to take you with me . . ." A kiss. "What did your man do to get such a fine woman like you . . ." A kiss.

Hopping back in the limo, he would say, "See, it only takes a minute, but imagine how good they feel about themselves."

Take that philosophy a few steps further into the bedroom, and you can understand how Ali racked up records that will never be broken in the realm of the horizontal rhumba.

How did he do it? Sometimes before a big fight, you would pass ten or twenty women in line in the hallway outside his suite. I always told him he should pass out numbers like at a deli. So, physically, how did he do it?

Roberto Clemente, the late Pittsburgh Pirate superstar, was a pelvic marathon man of Ali proportions. Watching him go through a lineup of twelve Latin lovelies in Caracas one day before a doubleheader, I asked him how he did it.

"I don't have an orgasm," he said simply.

"So what good does it do you?"

"I keep the best one for last, and then, yes, I let go."

Beside helping him set the indoor Western Hemisphere record for priapism, I wondered what it did to Clemente's stamina for the game.

"Hey, it's only a muscle. We must exercise it."

Immediately I heard the voices of the Gray Men in my head:

"If you don't use it, you lose it."

So Ali and Clemente furnished more joyrides than the roller coaster in Disneyland.

Did Ali have serious affairs? A few. Some pregnancies? A few. Some bastard children? A few.

Again, Ali's generosity was overwhelming. A girl had only to call to say she was pregnant, and he would buy a house for her.

If all the girls who got houses from Ali were to live in a subdivision, they might make up a larger area than Allentown.

And if we are going to exhaust this subject, let us say that Ali never (to my knowledge) went with white girls. He turned down many a famous white actress and singer with a courtly, "No thank you, ma'am."

I cannot understand why anyone finds his personal life so un- usual in this world of rock stars and politicians and their raucous lives. Ali kept it simple. No drugs. No smoking. No drinking. He was simply a hearty man who couldn't say no to a lady. As the playwright Harvey Fierstein says: "I just want to be loved, or is that so wrong?"

Chapter 5

Religion

To understand the saga of Ali, and to appreciate his full personality, one must examine what religion meant to Ali, and how his fate and place in history is tied in to his beliefs.

The young Cassius Clay dutifully went to church with Odessa. Southern blacks had accepted the faith of their slave masters, and when their emancipation came, they continued in their belief in Christianity. The majority worshiped in Protestant churches, adding some residual African beliefs and bringing along their music and voices.

Young Cassius Clay was subjected to racial tirades at home from his father, but went to church on Sunday and worshiped a white Jesus, Mary, Joseph, St. Peter, and the Apostles. The only black man his Bible recorded was Balthazar, one of the three wise men.

While Cassius Clay trained diligently for his first big test, the fight with Sonny Liston, he and his younger brother Rudy were quartered in the Overtown area of Miami. Rudy had free time, and he chose to spend it at Red's Barbershop, where the conversation was always lively.

Now the main speaker at Red's was a man known as Cap'n Sam,

who had run some numbers in his day, booked some horse bets, shined shoes, and was the main recruiter for a new religion, the Black Muslims. They were regarded with great doubt by the blacks of Overtown, and with suspicion and fear by the whites of segregated Miami.

Rudy Clay, an impressionable young man, deeply influenced by his father's railings against the evils of the white man, was an easy target for Cap'n Sam, and it was not long before he signed on. Cap'n Sam, who knew the world of sports, was actually after bigger game. He knew that if he signed Cassius Clay and Clay became champion, it would be a mighty boost for the Black Muslims. Cap'n Sam taught Rudy well, and then began a campaign to recruit Cassius Clay.

Like Rudy, Cassius was unhappy in the world of the South— and the North, as he had found out, was not much better. How could he return in triumph from Rome, holding his gold medal, and be stopped from eating in a restaurant in Louisville? The white man was not to be trusted. He loved you for your athletic prowess, but hated you for the color of your skin. This was unfathomable to a young man whose heart was full of love, who was gentle and kind, who avoided confrontations.

The world of the Overtown ghetto was equally confusing to a young boy brought up in a middle-class home. Clay did not understand gang wars, thefts, dope, womanizing, depravity, and poverty. He did not "fit."

When the young Cassius Clay stepped into the Sir John Bar to hear the wondrous music and watch the exciting dancing (Clay, in spite of his great athletic ability, did not dance), he was viewed as a target.

"What do you want, kid?" they'd ask, flashing gold-toothed smiles. "Want a drink? Vodka? Scotch? Wine?"

"No, thanks, I'm in training to fight the Bear. I'm going to be the Heavyweight Champion of the Whole Wide World!"

"I saw you looking at the Geechie's high, tight ass. You want her?"

"No, thanks. In training."

"Some ladies round here been dying to say hello . . ."

"Umm, no, thanks . . . in training."

"I guess dope is out of the question . . ."

Soon, the ghetto adopted him. It protected him, and it wanted this innocent, handsome young god to win. Wanted the world to know he came out of Overtown, well fed, well protected, and rested, sin-free as the day he was born.

When Cassius listened to Rudy's excited babble about a movement which called white people "blue-eyed devils," which espoused separatism, and which advocated a free, self-sustaining black nation of Islam, with its own nonwhite religion that was full of talk about Allah and the Koran and full of miracles that the black man had performed, Cassius was hooked.

Jubilation reigned in Red's little barbershop, as Cap'n Sam received the news and started his indoctrination course. Cassius was openmouthed in wonderment. Here was a religion which said that not only is black the best race, it's the *only* race. Blacks, or rather nonwhites, form a huge part of the earth's population, and Muslims outnumber Christians, so it appeared to Cassius Clay that he had joined a championship religion.

The first thing to do was get rid of his slave name: Cassius Marcellus Clay became Muhammad Ali. The name game became dicey, because all of the world knew Cassius Clay, the Louisville Lip. No one knew what a Muhammad Ali was.

The names bear inspection. Cassius Marcellus Clay was the name of an abolitionist who had actually freed, but kept, his slaves, and was reported to have boxed with one named George. From this unique man, the Clay family evolved.

Muhammad Ali was not just a name chosen by the Honorable Elijah Muhammad, it was a *title*, and it meant "worthy of respect and beloved of Allah." What this clearly showed was that Elijah knew very well what a valuable jewel had fallen into his lap. To him, Ali spelled credibility and respectability.

A brief, if telescoped, history of the Black Muslims will help the reader to better understand their attraction for an impressionable young fighter trying to find a way in life, one compatible with the requirements of his profession, his race, and his manhood.

The Honorable Elijah did a stretch of time in a federal penitentiary in Atlanta because of income tax evasion. He was a studious man, given to reading and meditation. It was here that a concept, based on an Eastern religion and adapted to the needs of racial separation, thus appealing to the repressed black masses, took hold. Incubated. Baked.

When Elijah was released, he founded the Black Muslim movement. His first converts were cons, and when he began to build his tough organization, those cons formed the storm-troop wing called the Fruit of Islam. Convicts, upon release, now had a place to go. The only difference in Elijah's organization was that the frail old man expected—no, demanded—that his followers *believe*, and *obey*. He was strict. If he used force, it was to do good, to correct wrongs. The Muslims were scrupulously honest. Gangsterism was a way of the past; Elijah was on a crusade, and once you *got* in, you *stayed* in, and did it Elijah's way.

Cassius Clay marched to his own drummer, and no one felt he could be controlled, told what to do, told to obey. Not even Elijah could harness this shooting star. When ordered to do something, Ali would nod his head, acquiesce, then go on his way. But skeptics were wrong. Ali believed. Believed deeply. He was a ship adrift, rudderless, without a captain, but now, listening to the wisdom of this old man, Ali saw the way. The road was dark, but it was illuminated by the Light of Knowledge, a light emanating from the Honorable Elijah Muhammad.

Once I rode through a hot, humid Miami summer night in my antique '47 Cadillac convertible with the top down and Ali in the backseat, his arms around two adoring girls. Suddenly, Ali tapped my shoulder and ordered me to pull over. He stood in the backseat, his handsome face beaming, one long muscled arm extended heavenward, pointing at a twinkling star.

"See that?" he said to the girls in a hushed tone. "It's the spaceship."

"What spaceship is that?" one of the girls asked. "The *Enterprise*?"

Ali looked at her as if she had come from another galaxy. I knew we were in for a Muslim indoctrination lecture.

"One day, 'bout six thousand years ago, a bad, mad scientist named Dr. Yakub grafted the white race *off* the black . . ."

It was Darwin's Theory of Evolution, Leakey's anthropological findings on the origins of man (the first man was from Africa), and Flash Gordon.

"The mad doctor made the whites superior, and pushed the blacks down into slavery. That period is coming to an end now."

"What's that got to do wid a spaceship? The *Enterprise II?*" asked the "Star Trek" groupie.

"Well, a spaceship took off with twenty-six yellow families living on it, circling the globe. They called it the Mothership. The mission is that if the nonwhite races are being oppressed by the whites, they will come down and wipe out the white race."

"What they been waiting for, chile?" asked the older of the two girls.

Ali ignored the question, continuing on, as if trying to complete the entire speech without a pause.

"Once a year they come down on the North Pole, put down a big plastic hose, and scoop up enough oxygen and ice to last them a year."

Ali looked skyward, and pointed: "The Mothership," he said reverentially.

Both girls understood that he was serious, and, thankfully, did not make fun of the story.

One of the main foundations of the government's case against Muhammad Ali was that he alleged he was a Muslim minister. He was Muslim, all right, but a minister? Had he trained to be a minister? Could anyone be a minister? When had Ali had time to train, to receive instruction? Did he practice his ministry? If so, where? When? How?

So it was that one humid night two neatly dressed FBI agents visited me in my Overtown clinic. Exhausted by a long day in the clinic, I eyed them warily as they presented their credentials and sat down.

"Have you personally ever been to a mosque, and have you heard Ali speak and preach?"

"Are you guys *new* on this case? Can you imagine *me* in a mosque?

"Well, have you ever heard him preach?"

I repeated the Mothership story. They laughed. I might as well

have been reading from an old television script. I maintained a
stony face.

"You don't believe any of that drivel, do you?"

"If you have faith, you can believe anything."

"But a Mothership? Yellow families . . . ?"

They were doubled over with laughter.

"Are you gentlemen religious?" I asked.

"Yes."

"Christians?"

"Yes."

"Then you believe that a man called Jonah got into a whale's
stomach and stayed for days, then came out safe and sound?

"You believe in the burning bush?

"You believe the Red Sea parted?

"You believe in the Immaculate Conception?

"You believe in the dead returning?

"You believe in the story of the wine and the loaves of bread?

"You believe Noah built an *ark* and that that ark held all species
of living matter?

"If you *believe* your Bible, why do you find it funny that Ali
believes *his* scripture?"

Good-bye, FBI.

Suffice it to say that in the matter of religion, Ali once again
picked intuitively the one that fitted his needs best. The bottom
line, now that his career is at an end, is that the Muslims were as
good for Ali as Ali was good for them. Symbiosis at its purest.

The gains for the Muslims were obvious. Their credentials were
established. They were finally credible as a religion.

For Ali, the gain was equally good. First, he got spiritual direction, which he was sorely lacking. Then strict dietary laws, all of
them blending nicely with the requirements of a boxer's training
routine. Then moral guidance: no drinking, smoking, dope, or
wenching. Failing on only one of four—wenching—wasn't bad.
The Muslims provided protection from whites of all types (except
that Ali had a white trainer, Angelo Dundee, and a white doctor,
me)—and protection from white women. And, most important of
all, he had a strong commander in Elijah Muhammad.

Did Ali for once toe the mark? Well, more or less. No one has ever successfully told Ali what to do. He listens, he nods, then he does what *he* wants to do.

He had a great love for Elijah, and mostly he did as he was told. After all, the Vietnam thing was not political, it was religious, ordered by Elijah. I know of few men who would risk all they have worked so hard to obtain, who would risk censure, calumny, and incarceration, on the orders of one feeble old man.

Ali did. Case closed. Ali was, and still is, a religious man, and Allah is his god.

Chapter 6

Ali the Man—An Appreciation

It is difficult to appreciate and understand the fights of Muhammad Ali unless one attempts to understand Ali, the man.

Based on close observation of his behavior over thirty years, I have drawn only one conclusion: Ali, the three-time heavyweight champion, was the best fighter I have ever seen. This is not hard to believe. Ali, the man, is so good, so special, so unique, that he *is* hard to believe.

Ali's life is exemplary. He is devoted to his mother and father, protective of his younger brother. His athletic career is one of the great sagas of sports. Motivation speakers salivate when they recite his characteristics.

Goal-motivated, his eye was always firmly fixed on the heavyweight championship.

Able to overcome adversity, he wins and loses the title three times; loses to the United States government in court and momentarily becomes disgraced, but comes back to prove himself a

44

folk hero because he is willing to go to jail for his beliefs. He marries four times, sires six children, yet he remains highly admired by society.

A *fanatic believer* of Islam, he is nonetheless accepted by all, and admired as a man with the guts to stand by his religious beliefs.

The list goes on: *Generous* to a fault, Ali cannot say *no* to any petitioner. Forgiving to his own who are caught stealing, for he cannot bear to hurt anyone. *Loving*, so that he cannot stand to reject people who care for him. *Nonviolent*, he's a peaceful man who hates violence outside the ring; even in the ring, he is not a killer puncher like Dempsey, Louis, Marciano, Liston, Foreman, or Tyson. His style is more like fencing than doing battle with a broadsword.

Now, at fifty, Ali still is a remarkable man—his life falling into soft focus; his qualities, once obscured by the bombast and blaring trumpets of the high-flying Ali Circus, now muted; his chatterbox, rapid-fire doggerel no longer delivered in an electric voice, but spoken in a deep rumble, slowly and hesitantly. The animated, childlike, gleeful, mischievous face of the young champion is now round and flat, emotionless, the facial nerves no longer transmitting their rapid orders to muscles that then translate them to expression. No quick smile now, no comic leer, no surprised looks, no resigned scowls, but rather a moon face. A middle-aged, flat face masking the ticking mind of a young Ali. For the mind works. The mind behind the mask is working, but the wires are down to the outside world. What an irony! What a ghastly price to pay for staying "on" too long, for pleasing the public, for giving it, and all of us, what we wanted: the Ali Circus to ride on forever. We thought he would never grow old, would never slow down, would never stop being fun—would never stop being Ali.

Boxing is a tough master. It does not forgive. Ruthlessly, it makes anyone who stays on too long pay the price. That penalty is stiff. There is no reprieve, only a bill that compounds annually, faster than an IRS debt. And boxing makes them all pay, whether a journeyman fighter from Tijuana or the greatest champion of all time.

But, fellow fans, sing no sad songs for Ali. As he has done all his days, he lives a contented life. *He* accepts his penalty. He knows he has to pay the piper, and so he adjusts. This is another part of the role he has been playing on earth. Now, he is Ali, the retired fighter. Happily married, living on a peaceful farm outside Detroit, roaming the world as a goodwill ambassador for his religion, for boxing, and for his race. He is an object of veneration. He is a man to be envied. He is a man with great inner peace. He has received the harvest of love from the seeds he sowed in his twenty years of world travel.

He emerges from any examination as a true individualist. There is only one Ali. He is unique. He is *unico*. If Frank Sinatra can sing "I Did It My Way," then Ali should have an opera dedicated to him. It should be entitled "The Greatest Fighter of All Time!"

Chapter 7

Ali the Act—An Appreciation

When Ali (still Cassius Clay) came home from Rome with a gold medal around his neck, he was a young man in need of guidance, of financial security, of being "moved" at the *right* pace by top professionals into the tricky but profitable world of professional boxing.

In his hometown of Louisville, Bill Faversham, a millionaire sportsman, rounded up a group of investors and took over the career of Cassius Clay. The Louisville Sponsoring Group, as it came to be known, negotiated with Cassius Senior and wrote a strict, tough contract, which, among other things, provided for a trust fund that could not be touched until young Cassius reached thirty-five years of age. This provided Cassius Clay with his first feeling of security, and a taste of riches to come.

During this gestation period, Angelo Dundee brought his smooth-boxing light heavyweight contender, Willie Pastrano, to Louisville to train for a few days, and Cassius Clay, already a stu-

dent of the slide-and-glide school of boxing, offered to work with
Willie.

Willie Pastrano had a slick style based on movement and a lightning jab, and he was propelled by fear. Maybe anxiety is a better
word, for once Willie was in the ring, he had a lion heart. In
addition to these qualities, Willie was wonderfully funny.

Cassius Clay jumped at the chance to work with a boxer he
greatly admired and the opportunity to show off his skills to a
trainer of Angelo Dundee's stature. Once the bell rang, Cassius
went into overdrive and boxed at a blinding speed, overwhelming
the surprised older fighter. After a single round of a one-sided
demonstration of boxing skill and speed, Willie wisely called a halt
to the sparring.

"Where did they get that kid?" Willie asked Angelo, who must
have been salivating over what he had just seen.

Luck, fortune, destiny, serendipity—call it what you will, but
all his life, Muhammad Ali has been at the right place at the right
time. He has been one of those people whom fate has chosen.

So when Cassius Clay most needed professional direction and
teaching, he fell into the hands of the hottest trainer-manager in
boxing. Faversham hastened to sign up Angelo Dundee, offering
him a nice deal: 10 percent of the fighter or $125 a week.

At this time, Angelo was still known as the younger brother of
Chris Dundee, the famous boxing promoter-manager, and they
formed a wonderful partnership, which was more Chris's brains
and Angelo's muscles.

Chris had not seen what Angelo had in the Pastrano workout,
and his opinion of Cassius Clay was the general consensus of opinion of the boxing cognoscenti: "Bad boxing habits, runs too much,
no punch, a loud mouth, and a wise guy. He'll get killed in the
pros."

With that as a basis for his decision, Angelo opted to take the
sure $125 a week over the ephemeral 10 percent of a kid who
would not last long in the world of the pros.

Angelo brought Clay to the mecca of boxing learning, the Fifth
Street Gym in Miami Beach, got him a room at the Mary Elizabeth
Hotel on Second Avenue in Overtown, and started his course of
training. It was here that the definitive Cassius Clay was born. He

was taught about the pro life with a great deal of gym humor by Willie Pastrano, and taken in with brotherly affection by top contenders like Gomeo Brennan and Luis Rodriguez. Cassius fell easily into the work of the gym.

But the Louisville Lip could not be silenced. He milked every bit of action into news stories. Ingemar Johansson was in training to fight Floyd Patterson for the third time. He came to Miami Beach, and Angelo craftily suggested to him that he box a few rounds with a young amateur fresh from the Olympics. Ingemar said yes, and the first chapter of Luck on the Ali Express was written—with the help of the writers who'd been tipped off.

If Clay surprised Pastrano, he absolutely stunned Ingemar. As they say in the gym: "He [Ingemar] never laid a glove on him."

As Pastrano had, Ingemar cut the workout short, and left in a huff, muttering (in Swedish, no doubt), "Who was that kid?"

The newspapers covered the rout nicely, it made the wires, and the Louisville Lip had scored his first hit.

One of the main ingredients of "the Act" was that Clay genuinely loved to "shock and amaze you." Like a kid showing off in front of adults, Clay loved to find an unusual thing to do, to create strange events, to behave in the exact opposite way expected of him. To be irrational, but to be amusing, entertaining. To challenge. To provoke. To irritate. To put himself out on a limb, then saw it off, and still prevail. This was his way to worldwide celebrity.

His first formal thoughts about the synthesis of his persona came after a visit to Gorgeous George in Las Vegas.

Gorgeous George was the most successful wrestler in the country. He dyed his hair a Marilyn Monroe blond; he came into the ring with a dresser, whose job it was to take the curlers out of George's blond hair, comb it out, and spritz it with hair spray, then help George out of his sequined robe and spray him with perfume from a gigantic atomizer—after which George would go out and beat the hell out of his opponent. Clay's eyes were wide as they took in this spectacle. He noted that the place was sold out and that half the people loved Gorgeous George and half hated him.

After the show, a rapt Clay listened as George gave him a lecture on showmanship.

"You gotta have a gimmick, kid. You got your good looks, a great body; they tell me you can fight like a dream, and you can talk even better than you can fight. You've got your act; now you need to polish it. Always dress in white. White robe, trunks, and shoes. Especially white shoes . . . makes you look even faster, and it'll make the purists hate you."

In those days boxers wore black or dark trunks, and definitely black shoes. The perfect role model for a champion was Joe Louis. Humility was a quality much appreciated in American heroes. A champion didn't brag outside the ring, but let his fists speak for him in the ring. A champion was a model of decorum. A champion was circumspect.

"Did you see the crowd out there? Half of 'em want to kiss me, half of 'em want to see me get killed. That is what you want. They all pay ten bucks to see what they want, but the bottom line is asses in the seats at ten bucks a pop.

"Now, you've got a great mouth. Lots of people love your brash, cocky style, and a lot of people will pay to see someone shut your mouth with a leather glove. So, keep on bragging, keep on sassing . . . and always be outrageous."

Cassius Clay was never short on creative originality, so, inspired by the lessons imparted by the flamboyant Gorgeous George, he came up with a gimmick. Clay would predict the round in which he would knock out his opponent. His early opponents were easy, so his predictions were accurate. The press soon picked up on it, and whether he was right or wrong in his predictions, he still got all the ink.

This was outrageous stuff, and it worked wonders when he made it come true. Out of this evolved doggerel rhymes using his opponent's name. "Moore in four," he would cry, and ancient Archie Moore would go down in four rounds. The public ate it up.

By March 1963, when he had a serious test at the hands of Doug Jones in Madison Square Garden, Clay had won seventeen pro fights in a row. He was highly ranked, and was in line for a title shot. In New York City, with its vast media coverage, Clay was in heaven. Until this point, he had traveled with a small group. Angelo Dundee used a varying group of assistants in the corner who came and went at Clay's whim. He had not yet found a kindred spirit, someone who understood his method, someone who could relate to his blackness, who could add to his unique flair.

Again Ali's Luck came into play. Fate stepped through the door in the form of Drew Bundini Brown.

Drew was part of the underworld of Harlem. He was an example of what Duke Ellington used to call "the Night People." Drew was a hustler with a heart, a broad poetic streak, and a sensitivity that he hid behind a screen of bluster. He was also an industrial-strength follower. He was a Sancho Panza looking for his Don Quixote.

Tall, imposing, and good-looking, Drew had traveled during the war to the Far East, and there had discovered the "mysteries of the East." He was full of mumbo jumbo, full of con laced with religious psycho-babble. Before platoons of motivational speakers invaded America's banquet halls, Drew was a prime motivational speaker. He talked his Harlem jive talk while fixing you with his hypnotic stare, and he was hard to resist.

Drew had been on the fringe of the Sugar Ray Robinson entourage, and this gave him the credentials with which to approach Cassius Clay, who considered Robinson the greatest fighter around.

Angelo Dundee, who likes to keep his camp orderly and sensible, was used to Clay attracting fruitcakes, and had developed a passive acceptance of their presence. Clay seemed to have an inner censor who went along with their eccentricities to a point, then cut them off when they got too rambunctious.

Drew moved into Clay's hotel, into his room, and ultimately into his heart. Clay had found a soul brother, and a slave, albeit a rebellious one. Drew was to become the author of Clay's most famous chant:

> Float like a butterfly,
> Sting like a bee,
> Rumble, young man, rumble,
> Aaaaaaaaaaaaagh!

He brought a quality of irreverent fun and rebellion to camp.

He understood what Clay required, and provided it. Drew Bundini
Brown became part cheerleader, part witch doctor.

Now, the Act was almost complete: Cassius almost always
dressed in white. (He added tassels to his shoes later.)

Cassius spouted doggerel at the snap of a camera.

Cassius nicknamed each opponent—Patterson (the Rabbit), Liston (the Bear), Foreman (the Mummy), Frazier (the Gorilla).

Cassius now had chants and yells and worked out routines with
Bundini.

Cassius made fun of the media and kept up a running, make-
believe feud with Howard Cosell, who benefited greatly from this
exposure.

Cassius became an instrument of vengeance in the ring. He
carried Floyd Patterson, tormenting "the Rabbit" for refusing to
call him Ali after his conversion. For the same slight, he punched
Ernie Terrell silly, yelling "What's my name?" with every jab.

It has always been part of Ali's life that he chooses an apparently
self-destructive road, only to have it turn out to be the right one.
Certainly, choosing to turn Muslim on the eve of the first Sonny
Liston fight in Miami Beach in 1964 was perceived by the press
and public as suicidal. It killed the box office. Ali almost had to
walk away from his most important fight because the promoters
wanted him to keep quiet about his religious conversion until afterward. Cassius Clay, a.k.a. Muhammad Ali, went into the Liston
fight as one of the most disliked contenders since Max Schmeling
had fought Joe Louis in 1938. It turned him from a hero to a villain
in one headline.

Shock and amaze 'em!

But it worked out, as all Ali's apparently self-destructive decisions have. Ali's luck always holds. The public had no sooner di-
gested the Black Muslim caper than Muhammad Ali, in 1967, announced he wasn't going to Vietnam, explaining, "I ain't got
nothing against no Vietcong."

Shock and amaze you?

There followed three years of hard exile, with precious few re-
maining loyal to Ali. Drew, Angelo, and the boxing crowd, appre-
ciative of boxing greatness, innocent in political affairs, hung in
with Ali. The press, except for an isolated voice like Howard Co-

Floyd Patterson scores briefly before being TKOd in the seventh round, New York, September 1972. *Photo courtesy AP/Wide World Photo*

sell, shunned him. But Ali hung on, kept his act alive by appearing on Broadway in a short-lived play (*Buck White*), did speaking engagements, and survived.

The government's position weakened as the public began to lose faith in a bloody, unpopular war. Television brought the war, with its needless brutality, into the nation's living rooms, and more and more youths burned their draft cards or went north to Canada. Ali's position became more and more acceptable, and attorneys scrambled to present the Supreme Court with a defensible case for him.

In the end, the Supreme Court ruled in favor of the fighter. Suddenly, Ali was free to fight, to go out and win back his title, now held by Smokin' Joe Frazier. Promoters ran hither and yon trying to find a state that would accept draft dodger Ali. It was only fitting, in keeping with Ali's bizarre luck, that it was the state of Georgia, with its rabid segregationist governor, Lester Maddox, that gave Ali the chance to take his first step forward in his quest to regain the title.

On October 26, 1970, Muhammad Ali stopped Jerry Quarry on cuts in the third round. The Act was back!

It was during the first Ali-Frazier fight in New York that the Act expanded and solidified.

The Ali Circus was born in Madison Square Garden that night. Hundreds of hard-living high-wire artists now began to attach themselves to Ali's star. Ali, with his love of humanity and his curiosity about the Night People, started taking them on his jaunts. With the advent of fights to Third World countries, the Ali Circus burgeoned, for these countries invariably had nationalized airlines that sent eighty to one hundred first-class tickets, and this was an invitation to the people waiting to work their way into the Ali Circus.

The Act lasted a long time, and Ali became a legend, his feats not likely to be equaled, his fun and merriment not to be missed, and his Ali Circus impossible to duplicate.

What was it about Ali that allowed him to be taken advantage of by so many freeloaders? Why did he let the Muslims dictate a stance that virtually wrecked his career? Why was he so patient with the ladies and their demands? Why did he fight as he did, in

A young mustached Ali. *Photo courtesy Hy Simon*

an almost balletic style? How did he cope so well with his critics? With his enemies?

The observation on the Act is that it is an act of a pure passive-aggressive personality.

Passive-aggressive types do not initiate action; instead they react to action. They manipulate. They make things happen by reacting to things people do to them (usually after these people have been manipulated into doing them), and so control their destinies in what appears to be a nonaggressive manner.

Thus Ali would accept a man into camp, then furnish him with enough rope to hang himself. Thus he joined the Muslims, but ended up living according to his interpretation of the rules. Thus Angelo Dundee appeared to plan his fights, but Ali fought them his way. Thus Herbert Muhammad made his managerial decisions, but Ali took what he wanted and left what he didn't want.

But no matter what yardstick you measure the Act by, it was, pure and simple, one of a kind—authored by Ali, acted out by Ali, and stamped by his unique personality.

It was, in the final analysis, a great act, the best ever seen in sports, and its was guaranteed to "shock and amaze you!"

BOOK TWO

Boxing Tour, the Ali Circus

Chapter 8

Cassius Clay: The Learning Process

Angelo Dundee had not signed on officially until after Cassius Clay's first bout, in October of 1960, with Tunney Hunsaker, a tough, white heavyweight. The bout went six rounds, and after it was in the record books, Bill Faversham closed his deal with Dundee. It was arguably the best move Clay ever made.

Dundee in the sixties was at the head of the line of manager-trainers in big-time boxing. With superhuman effort, he had created a stable of top contenders and champions. Angelo also had a great connection in Havana who fed him quality Cuban fighters fleeing from Fidel Castro. Angelo was overworked and he loved it. If ever a man loved his work, he was that man.

Cassius Clay had been sent to Archie Moore and trainer Dick Sadler by the Louisville Sponsoring Group at the very beginning, but Archie believed in starting at the bottom—sweeping floors, making beds, washing dishes, and cleaning up the gym. Cassius Clay believed in starting at the top. End of partnership.

Cassius Clay liked Angelo, idolized Willie Pastrano, and followed Luis Manuel Rodriguez's fights. One night Cassius carried Luis's bag into the fight arena. "That way I don't have to buy no ticket," said the irrepressible Clay.

"I'll take your bag, Mister Cuban Champion."

"That's nice, Mister Gold," said Luis, who had taken Clay under his wing.

So Angelo began what should go down in boxing history as the best-planned teaching career in the history of matchmaking, training, and the advancement of a fighter. To make fights that provide learning experiences, that increase your fighter's reputation, and that nonetheless possess the element of danger, is a fine art. In Ali's career, as in Jimmy Ellis's and Sugar Ray Leonard's, Angelo showed his Hall of Fame talent.

Ali's faults were obvious, but Angelo knew better than to try to make wholesale changes. His style was to take a boxer's natural

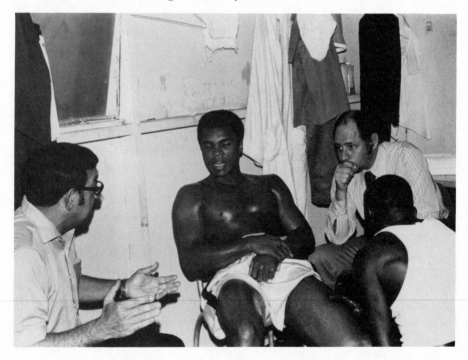

A bull session with the author and Angelo Dundee. *Photo courtesy Luisita Pacheco*

talent and make it better. Ali's faults would work for him because of his great natural ability, his physique, superior reflexes, and great confidence. Angelo understood that the Clay way was the right way. He also used his big-time fighters to help him perfect the Cassius Clay fighting machine. Daily work with Pastrano and Rodriguez honed his skills. Clay was being taught, although he didn't exactly realize it. I am sure that even today he is not aware of the amount of teaching and learning that he absorbed in that important gestation period in the Fifth Street Gym. That is precisely the value of the Dundee method. Fighters are developed in a loving camaraderie and end up thinking that they learned it all on their own. It was also to Clay's liking that Dundee never bragged or took credit for helping to create Cassius Clay, but stood aside like a doting father, deferring to the kid's rapidly growing fame. At first, Dundee had the name, and the press flocked to him for quotes, but skillfully he deflected the attention to the Louisville Lip. Cassius's mouth got the press, and his fists confirmed his boasts. Fade out Angelo Dundee, fade in Cassius Clay. Shouts of "I am the Greatest!" could be heard throughout the land.

Cassius Clay's career started on October 29, 1960 in Louisville, with that six-round decision over Tunney Hunsaker. The teaching fights continued with great success in 1961, but Clay hit his first bump on February 10, 1962, when he met Sonny Banks in New York City. By now, the media was churning out reams of publicity on this audacious kid who not only loudly proclaimed "I am the Greatest!" but had started calling the round in which he was going to knock out opponents.

Sonny Banks was a banger, and he represented another step up on Angelo's ladder of experience. Clay called the round again — round four. The press ate it up; Madison Square Garden was packed. A full house in the Garden can cause a young boxer to freeze up, and indeed Clay looked a little tense in round one. He had launched his climb-out-on-a-limb philosophy, and this represented his first real test. He was a 5–1 favorite; he had predicted a fourth-round knockout. The wise guys along Jacob's Beach and the Gray Men of the New York gyms could hardly wait to see if the kid would produce.

The first round nearly proved fatal, as Clay stood in front of

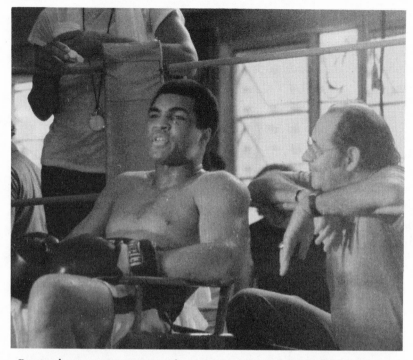

Resting between sparring rounds on the movie set of *The Greatest. Photos courtesy Luisita Pacheco*

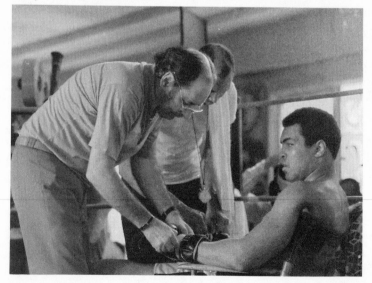

Banks, not giving him angles or lateral movement. Banks landed a solid left hook, and down went Clay!

Up at the count of two, Clay took an eight count before Banks came in to try to finish him off, Angelo studied his fighter's face. "Now we'll see what this kid is made of," Angelo thought. "Now we'll see what's ticking in his chest."

Cassius Clay's face showed more astonishment and embarrassment than pain or confusion. He snapped out of his trance and began to box, winning the rest of the round. In round two, he opened up his offense and decked Banks. Clay played with him after that, waiting until round four. The Garden went wild as that round arrived and Clay calmly knocked Banks out.

"I told you—I am the Greatest!" Clay bragged to the impressed

media that crowded around him, and even the hardest of the Gray
Men shuffled out into the cold New York night grudgingly admit-
ting that maybe, just maybe, Angelo Dundee had found himself a
fighter.

Cassius Clay rolled through 1962 with six KO wins over increasingly tough opposition, culminating in an impressive fourth-round
knockout of his first mentor, Archie Moore.

"Moore in four," he crowed to the Los Angeles scribes, and so
it happened. A few of the more cynical cried "Fix," but Clay had
clearly established himself with the fans, media, and Hollywood
movie crowd. Cassius Clay was a name on everyone's lips.

Angelo Dundee now decided to slow down and consolidate
Clay's position. Cassius Clay must not, Angelo felt, step up too
quickly to the absolute top of his class. He began with a tough
opponent in Charlie Powell, and Clay had no trouble stopping him
in the predicted third round.

Fans of boxing on television had taken to a small heavyweight
named Doug Jones, who could box well and was tough to hurt.
Each test on Professor Dundee's ring curriculum got harder, and
Clay's bout against Jones on March 13, 1963, would be his toughest
yet. Once again it was in the Garden, and once again Clay was out
on a limb. New York, with its aggressive population and press, and
Madison Square Garden, with its long history of boxing excellence,
had always bothered Cassius Clay. Normally unflappable before
any fight, he insisted on arriving two and a half hours early for this
one. This did not sit well with Angelo, who watched helplessly as
the anxious Clay worked out in his dressing room for the full two
and half hours.

Doug Jones was a small, compactly built, energetic heavyweight.
Clay was tense and, after two and a half hours of dressing room
exercise, sluggish. The fight was very close. Many thought Doug
Jones had won. The judges gave it to Cassius Clay, beginning a
pattern of close calls that was to be repeated throughout his career.

This was to be the first of many fights where Clay's overwhelming reputation gave the judges a slightly biased view. It is a phenomenon well known in boxing. Joe Louis received a few gifts in
his career, as did Sugar Ray Robinson and many others. It is the
way in boxing, and the one person who knew in his heart that

Cassius Clay had enjoyed an early Christmas was Angelo Dundee, although Gestapo torture would not have been able to get him to admit it. But back at the drawing board, Angelo saw clearly how well his fighter had progressed. Aside from the wins, the popularity, and the advancement of his boxing skills, Clay had shown a cool head. Against Jones he had shown patience, had overcome sluggishness, had learned not to leave his fight in the dressing room. In his quiet way, Angelo had crafted a complete fighting machine. Now, it was time to take the machine overseas and show the world this new wonder.

If there is a definitive point at which Cassius Clay became a full-fledged contender for the heavyweight championship, it was the Henry Cooper fight in London on June 18, 1963.

Henry Cooper ("Our 'Enery," the masses called him) was a top contender. He had a wicked left hook and knocked out most opponents. His weakness was his susceptibility to cuts. He bled profusely in every fight, and only his punching power saved him from losing many matches.

Spurred on by the British press and fans, Cassius Clay finally went too far and alienated them by calling their beloved Henry Cooper a "bum." And to add insult to injury, Clay entered the stadium wearing a jeweled crown and royal robes. The Brits love their royalty, and they saw this as an insult. The boos and whistles rained down on a shocked Cassius Clay. Clearly, he had crawled out on his accustomed limb and was busily sawing away. He added more fuel to the fire by predicting that he would knock out Cooper in five!

At the weigh-in, the cautious Angelo Dundee had done his usual thorough job of supervising the details of the bout, and he had noted and complained about the type of gloves to be used. They had a seam down the side, which Angelo felt was a weak point and could result in cuts. Since the fighter who figured to be cut was Cooper, Angelo did not press to change gloves, but insignificant as it seemed then, Angelo had spotted an opening. "For want of a nail . . ."

The fight started with Clay dancing and Cooper chasing. Nothing new there. By round four, Cooper was bathed in his own blood, the expected cut having been inflicted earlier by Clay's persistent snapping, popping jab. Things looked bleak for Cooper as the round was coming to a close.

Then something happened that stunned and surprised everyone, one of those solitary happenings that sometimes turns a fight around, turns victory into defeat.

Cooper, blinded by blood, started with a soft left jab, the sort of feel-'em-out, where's-he-located type of jab. A right hand usually follows. Clay, who had his hands down, taunting Cooper, turned instinctively to meet a right cross. But Cooper turned the jab into his patented explosive left hook. It crashed on Clay's jaw with the impact of a V-2 rocket, and down he went.

The crowd was in a frenzy as the referee began his count. When the count got to four, the bell rang, saving Clay by English rules. Cassius Clay got up on rubbery legs, his eyes glazed over, unseeing.

Now came one of those moments where one can assay the absolute value of a man. That man was not Cassius Clay, staggering around the ring, looking for his corner; that man was Angelo Dundee. So far I have described some of Angelo's assets, but where he really earned his money was in the corner. A great cornerman is a tactician, strategist, psychologist, physiotherapist, and motivator. When Angelo brought Clay to the corner, he needed a miracle to resuscitate his fighter and get him ready to face Cooper for round five. Clay's luck came into play. The first piece of luck was having Angelo; the second was having him spot a tear along the seams of Clay's gloves. Who but Angelo would have spotted a tear in a glove? In the middle of a sixty-second panic, who would have looked? Angelo did.

With a small bit of help from Angelo's finger, the tear is made worse. Angelo calls over the referee. Split glove. Can't continue. Teddy Waltham, secretary of the British Boxing Board of Control, confers with Tommy Little, the referee. The president of the boxing board is called in. "Nothing for it but to get a new glove," they agree. However, there isn't another pair in the stadium. Time, you will deduce, is ticking by. Angelo is giving Clay the smelling salt, putting cold water on his head, massaging his arms, making him shake his legs.

On the other side of the ring, they are so thankful for the time to do major surgery on Cooper's large cut that they forget to complain about the delay, during which Clay is recovering.

Alas, there are no other gloves. Round five must be fought with a damaged glove. Within a minute of round five, the referee stops the fight because Cooper is in danger of bleeding to death.

"Round five . . . I predicted it!

"I AM THE GREATEST!"

Cassius Clay hurriedly leaves the ring, *not* wearing his royal crown and robe. Luck has held up once again. Clay was lost, and Angelo had saved him.

A real bond was being forged between the two men. In his quiet way, Angelo Dundee was putting the final touches on his molding of a champion. Cassius Clay, the final product, was almost complete. Now there remained the final test: the heavyweight championship and the "big, ugly Bear," Sonny Liston.

Chapter 9

The First Coming: The Sonny Liston Fight

Cassius Clay launched a countrywide search for Charles "Sonny" Liston in order to taunt him into a fight for the title. Bundini and Howard Bingham, Clay's photographic Boswell, accompanied him, and it was a hilarious romp, with sophomoric Clay putting a bear trap on Sonny's lawn in Denver in the middle of the night, and with many another practical joke, calculated to get Liston mad enough to revert to homicide. It was well recorded in the press (Clay saw to that) and served its purpose well, for Sonny, finally weary of Clay's loud mouth and childish pranks, signed to fight on February 25, 1964, in Miami Beach.

In order to understand the extent of this accomplishment, the miracle of having Liston sign to fight the fresh young Ali, you have to understand what an unbeatable, tough, threatening, bestial champion Sonny Liston appeared to be. Clay vs. Liston was a boy vs. a man, youth vs. experience, good vs. evil, amateur vs. pro.

Liston opened a 6–1 favorite to win, 3–1 that he would kill Clay.

Sonny Liston was a big man, which led him easily into the life of an enforcer—a man who collected debts, or enforced contracts; a man whom no one wanted to see when times got tough.

Apparently in and out of correctional institutions, Sonny finally found lifetime employment with the help of a man known as Blinky Palermo, who along with Frankie Carbo represented the underworld in the fight game of the forties and fifties. Sonny lived in Blinky's house in Philly for a few years and began his boxing career in 1953 with a one-round knockout of a victim named Don Smith.

Sonny's road to the title was paved with one-round KOs, as he made it a habit to have short nights at the "office." By 1962, even the protective Cus D'Amato could not keep Sonny from getting a shot at Floyd Patterson's title. Floyd, a man of great pride and weak chin, overrode D'Amato's strident objections and signed to fight Sonny on September 25, 1962, in Chicago.

A student by nature, Floyd had studied the moth's strange behavior toward the flame, and apparently drawing the wrong conclusion from this aberrant behavior, he took the fight straight to Sonny Liston. Floyd fit his china chin to Liston's gigantic paw, and visited the canvas instantly. The place was empty by the time Floyd came to, found his disguise of dark glasses and fake beard, and skulked into the Chicago night.

Great was the rejoicing in some Italian restaurants around the country as Sonny Liston became the heavyweight champion of the world—and underworld. There was occasion to celebrate again when Floyd, exhibiting a world-class masochistic desire for punishment, insisted on a rematch.

Poor Floyd, a psychological basket case, studied films of the flame-to-the-moth first combat and deduced what the rest of the country already knew: He had frozen. So intent was Floyd *not* to freeze the next time around that he froze. Again. One round. Sonny was hailed as an unbeatable champ.

Now, Cassius Clay, the Louisville Lip, had finally taunted unbeatable Liston into a title fight. Once again, Clay was out on a limb, and once again, before the ink was dry on the contract, he started sawing away on that limb.

Bill Faversham and the Louisville Sponsoring Group had been good for Clay. They had paid him well, stayed discreetly in the background, hired Angelo Dundee, and finally, in view of the exceptional job he had done, named him Cassius Clay's official manager. Now, with the official opening of the training camp, came rumors that Clay was flirting with a fringe "lunatic" religion called the Black Muslims. Since Angelo had what is known nowadays as a "focused mind," he was not aware of Clay's outside activities, so it did not surface as a factor until the day before the fight—although the rumors had been as bad for the box office as the confirmation of them.

Chris Dundee had come up with an angel for the fight in Bill MacDonald, a millionaire sportsman. They had started out with a hot attraction: a bad guy against a good guy. Black hat against a white hat. A killer against a gold medal winner. Good vs. Evil. But if Clay had joined this racist group, the fight had become a non-attraction. Bad vs. Bad does not a box office sellout make.

Chris was getting killed at the box office, and Sonny Liston's cavalier attitude in training did not help any. Sonny trained mainly by having Willie Reddish fling a medicine ball against the flat Liston abdomen. Then he jumped rope to the slow blues beat of Coleman Hawkins's recording of "Night Train." If the mood struck him, Sonny would beat up some frightened sparring partners; then he'd come to the microphone and deadpan his one-liner: "I don't know what I'm training so hard for—this kid ain't gonna last one round."

Finally, he would have his picture taken with the fans for a buck a pop.

Meanwhile, the Fifth Street Gym was a beehive of activity. Every fan, every girl, every celebrity, every media person would jam into the place (at fifty cents a piece) to watch Cassius Clay work out.

Clay would skip rope gracefully before the ever-present mirror. Sweat gleaming off his slick, butter-colored skin, his long, smooth legs gracefully skipping, Clay would seem transfixed by what he saw in the mirror. Then perhaps there'd be a flashy, rapid exhibition of hitting the light bag, and then floor exercises, with the sad-eyed Cuban conditioner Luis Sarria working with him. Finally he'd mix it up with topflight sparring partners, ending up admin-

Chris Dundee. *Photo courtesy Luisita Pacheco*

istering a beating to brother Rudy, who was being persuaded to give up boxing.

By this time the gym was packed. Cameras were clicking, TV and movie crews were working. Clay would lean on the top rope and begin a rambling monologue, helped along by the resourceful Bundini, who could think up a new saying on a moment's notice.

The champ jumping rope. *Photo courtesy Luisita Pacheco*

The crowd ate it up, and it would have been a helluva gate had not the Muslim issue hung in the air. The rumor would not go away.

By the day of the weigh-in, Ed Pope of the *Miami Herald* was breaking the news that Cassius Clay had joined the Black Muslims. Chris saw his waterfall of dollars slow to a trickle of cheap-seat sales.

The weigh-in was a masterpiece of Clay psychological warfare. Up to this point everyone had tolerated his high jinks, but now a certain solemnity was in order. This was, after all, a fight for the heavyweight championship.

Clay had always admired Sugar Ray Robinson, and although the young fighter had been snubbed when he went to visit him in his bar in New York, Sugar still meant a great deal to Clay. So Angelo brought him in to add dignity to the proceedings. After all, Sonny Liston had brought *his* idol, Joe Louis, to be with him.

In the hallway, Clay and the entourage waited to be introduced. A meeting was taking place. A lecture was being given by Sugar Ray about the seriousness of the occasion, and Clay nodded. He agreed to everything told to him . . . until he hit the door. Then he and Bundini went into their war chants:

> Float like a butterfly,
> Sting like a bee
> Rumble, young man, rumble!
> Aaaaaaaaaaaaaaaaaaaaaaaaaa!

The crowd of photographers had a field day as Clay and Bundini attacked the dais in full fury. Angelo, Sugar Ray, and the rest followed helplessly. Liston and his crew looked on in amazement. Never had anyone shown Liston such disrespect. He tried glowering, but that just launched Clay on another verbal rampage.

Clay now stepped up to confront Liston, and played his trump card. He stood nose to nose with the big, bad Liston.

"I got you now, Sonny; I got your championship now!"

The trump card was that Liston was *looking up* to Clay. Clay was taller. And bigger! Liston always put extra towels on to look bigger—Lord knows why, since he had huge shoulders. Clay, because of his baby face and smooth, perfectly proportioned body, always looked smaller on film than he was in person. Clay's size seemed to deflate Liston, and he tried to make a feeble joke out of the entire affair. Clay screamed another bit of poetry.

It came time for the physical examination, and Clay sprang another shocker. Dr. Alexander Robbins found he was running a 200/100 blood pressure. Under normal rules, the fight would be called off. Robbins looked perplexed.

"What's happening, Doc?" asked the acerbic Jimmy Cannon, a feisty syndicated columnist from New York who was always looking to nail Clay. Robbins was busy looking at his *Merck Manual* under "Hypertension, Heavyweight," when Cannon, who had been writing that Clay was a coward and scared to death, sidled up to the doctor.

"Could it be that the kid is scared to death?" he taunted.

Dr. Robbins saw a blinding flash of light comparable to that of an atomic blast. It was a vision of an alibi coming forth, getting him off the hook.

"That's it! We'll give him this afternoon to calm down, then if it's normal, the fight is on."

The day before the weigh-in, Clay had insisted on announcing his conversion to the Muslim faith. The *Miami Herald*'s Ed Pope refused to print his Muslim name. Bill MacDonald, whose money was at risk, threatened to cancel the fight. Cassius Clay had worked so hard to get this chance at the title, yet he was prepared t risk it all for his religion. Clay was on the bus, ready to go home, /hen word came that the fight would go on. The world was about to see a fighter named Muhammad Ali.

Meanwhile, I had been ordered to go back to Ali's house and monitor his blood pressure. Angelo, Ali, and I entered the small house now packed with followers of the Fruit of Islam listening to tapes by Malcolm X exhorting them to kill the white devils. It was not a moment I would care to relive. I felt like a Jew at a Nuremberg rally.

Ali went to his room, where I took his blood pressure: 120/80. Entirely normal. Ali, who had been wild-eyed at the weigh-in, now looked cool and detached. He had a Gandhi-like serenity about him.

"Why did you do all that hysterical stuff? Why did you get your blood pressure up like that?"

"Because Liston is a bully, and a bully is scared of a crazy man. No one can tell what a crazy person is going to do. Now Liston thinks I'm crazy. I got him worried." He smiled, safe in the knowledge that on this night of nights he, Cassius Clay, who had become Muhammad Ali, held the edge.

So it was a quiet Muhammad Ali who went into the Miami Beach Auditorium dressing room and locked the door.

"Nobody in, nobody out" was the word the Fruit of Islam guards were given.

Inside were Ali, Rahaman (Rudy Clay), Bundini, cornerman Solomon McAteer, Angelo, and me. Angelo and I were the only white men present.

Ali took a water bottle wrapped in white tape, sealed with a signature on the tape, and gave it to Rahaman.

"Watch the bottle. Don't nobody take the tape off."

Poor Rahaman. He had to get ready for *his* fight, and he had to guard the bottle. Against what, one might ask, since we were all part of his family. Such was the nuttiness of that evening.

Rahaman went out to absorb his beating, and Ali slipped into the back of the hall to watch it. He swore he would never let his brother fight again. Rahaman did have a few more bouts, but Ali saw to it that he stopped and that he never had to worry about financial security again.

After an interminable wait, and a comic-opera shuffle while Ali and Rahaman tried to figure out which direction was east so they could utter their Muslim prayers, we were led out to the arena.

There were more people in the press section than there were at ringside. People were there mostly to see the big, ugly Bear shut Ali's big mouth.

Out of more than eight hundred newsmen, only eight had picked Ali. The only persons I knew who gave him a chance were Angelo, always a strong believer; Bundini and Solomon, who each had slipped me $100 to bet on Clay at 6–1; Sarria, who had great boxing acumen; and myself, who didn't know any better.

The first round was a surprise for the confident Liston and the crowd. Ali came out on flying feet, his jab popping Liston's head back as the Bear moved aggressively forward. Liston, for his part, almost ran after Ali. The rumor was that he had a heavy bet on himself to knock out Ali in *one*. If so, he went to his corner frustrated and considerably poorer.

Steve Ellis, doing blow-by-blow alongside Joe Louis, who was doing the analysis, speculated that Ali's speed was motivated by fear. The kid looked jittery, but he did win the first round.

Having survived the track meet of the first round, Ali settled down to a dull second round, again providing a surprise: he fought it in orthodox, hands-held-high style. It wasn't Ali. It wasn't good. He lost the round to a hard-charging, aggressive Liston, who was willing to eat a jab in order to land a thunderous body punch to Ali's side. Liston's round.

The third and fourth rounds were Ali at his best. Liston seemed discouraged and winded by his all-out effort. And even more discouraging than his inability to connect with the flashing Ali was the fact that his face was lumping up, cut and bleeding, and his shoulder was hurting. How could he know that the bell ending round four would be his last great chance to save his title?

Ali returned to his corner rubbing his left eye. It was red and throbbing, and he could not see. Again it was time to call on his luck, and again his luck was that Angelo Dundee was in his corner. Angelo went right to work on the eye, washing it out while talking calmly to his fighter.

Ali was anything but calm. He was in severe pain. He was blind. He was facing a killer. His life was in danger. Bundini, not the calmest man in the most serene of circumstances, was incoherently babbling: "I knew the white man would think of a way to trick us." Then Clay said, "Cut them off," extending his gloves. Fortunately, Bundini had no scissors.

The Muslims at ringside were getting surly and speculating on how Angelo had put the "stuff" on his sponge to blind Ali. Hearing the threats, another Dundee brother, Jimmy, who came to all the fights to help, rushed up and had Angelo wipe his own eyes to show that there was nothing on the sponge.

Meanwhile, the sixty seconds had ticked away and referee Barney Felix was walking toward the corner. The stool was taken out of the ring. Ali was standing, still blinking, and Angelo gave him

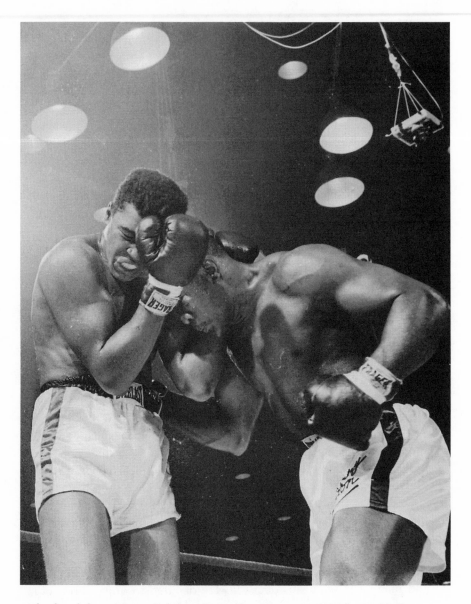

The first fight in Miami, February 1964. *Photo courtesy AP/Wide World Photos*

the *word*. "This is for the heavyweight championship; no one walks away from that. Get in there and run until your eyes clear up."

The bell sounded to start the fifth round. There was a pause as Ali faltered, but then he launched on his circuitous route, avoiding Liston, who was slow to catch on that his opponent could not see. When Liston finally understood that all he had to do was corner the blinded Ali and knock him out, he ran after him, throwing heavy punches in the air. But this probably did more to aggravate his shoulder injury than anything else. Liston later reported that he felt like his "arm was full of water."

Ali felt his eye clearing up by the end of the round, and as it ended, he was popping his jab and talking to Liston. Once again, Ali's luck had held.

Let's pause a moment here to evaluate this round and how Ali's luck always pulled him through critical, crossroad situations. What if Angelo had not been in his corner? What if a lesser man had been in charge? Ali would have quit—quit like the dog most people thought he was. What of the Muslim conversion? The prophet, the Honorable Elijah Muhammad, felt that *all organized sports* were evil and held his people to slave contracts. Prophets do not bend easily—after all, they're infallible; therefore, there had been an enormous amount of rationalization, philosophical tap-dancing, and smoke-blowing to allow Cassius Clay to convert. Yet if Ali was champion, the loss of face would be balanced out by the gain in the coffers. But, what of a man who quit in his corner? How would the Honorable Elijah take that? Had he quit like a dog, not even Malcolm X would have taken him in. As for the boxing fraternity, he would have been dead in the water. Box office poison.

So Muhammad Ali's career and life hung for a moment in the hands of this gentle, quiet little man whose competitive spirit, whose love of Ali, would not *let* him quit. Ali's luck. Always when he needed it.

Suddenly, at the end of the round, Liston went to his corner and made a momentous decision. He decided to quit. Bereft of a Dundee in his corner, weary, battered, his arm becoming useless, his eyes closing up, and with the sure knowledge that "there will be another night" (as Willy Reddish kept telling him), Sonny Liston handed over the heavyweight championship of the world. The bully had quit. The Louisville Lip had won. Pandemonium broke loose in the ring. Muhammad Ali climbed on the ring ropes, yelling over and over again, "I told you—I am *the Greatest!*"

And so he was.

Chapter 10

Lewiston: The Liston Rematch

Immediately after the shocker in Miami Beach all manner of things started to happen.

Cassius Clay's name went into the record books and out of usage. For all but a few die-hard writers, boxers, promoters, and fans, Clay became Muhammad Ali.

Ali was married to Sonji at the time, and there was already friction, in the form of her rebellious refusal to adhere to puritanical Muslim concepts of what women should look and dress like and how they should behave.

The Muslims moved into the boxing management field, and the Louisville Sponsoring Group felt itself being pushed to get out. It would take until 1966 for the Muslims to phase out the group and to replace Angelo Dundee with Elijah's son, Herbert Muhammad, as manager.

Meanwhile, inside the Fifth Street Gym, things went on as

usual. The mission now was to prepare to fight the Bear again. Many delays had occurred, but by early 1965, the fight was set.

Sonny Liston had a hard time accepting his loss of face. This time there would be no overconfidence, no lack of diligent training, no lack of a game plan. This time Liston would be *ready*.

Fight experts who saw him during this time said that they had never seen him look so good, and be so *ready*.

Liston, who was approaching thirty-six—although he didn't say from which side—was a bulky man, and could not maintain a tough training schedule for a long period of time.

So with Liston at his peak, with the fight date around the corner, the Ali luck came into play. Ali was diagnosed as having a hernia, and was whisked off to the hospital to have it fixed. This delay proved great for Ali, terrible for Sonny.

Sonny could not maintain his shape, his conditioning, for three months. He would have to quit and start again, or work in an easy fashion to try to maintain his edge—but this is not possible in an old fighter. His main edge was psychological. This mean man wanted revenge. Wanted it bad. Was ready to *hurt* this kid who had humiliated and embarrassed him—and now Ali had pulled another one of his stunts.

Ali, of course, came to Lewiston, Maine, refreshed and recharged, enjoying the considerable attention he was getting. Once again, he was out on a limb, sawing away.

Rumors were rife of Mafia gunmen out to kill Ali. Counterrumors of busloads of Fruit of Islam storm troopers descending on quiet Lewiston to impose their order and protect their Muslim champion caused the governor to send extra security.

In one of the first of the quixotic trips the Ali Circus was to take, the fighter bought an old Trailways bus, wrote his name on the side, hired a driver, and invited the press and the members of his camp to ride with him to Lewiston. Shades of Budd Schulberg's *The Harder They Fall*, of the bus with an El Toro cutout on the side and the publicity trip through the sticks.

That the route of the bus would take them through the heart of the segregated South seemed to amuse Ali.

The trip was a misadventure, as Drew Bundini Brown refused to acknowledge the fact of racial discrimination and confidently got off the bus and went into one bus stop cafe after another, only to meet the same treatment in each one. Ali found this funny. Brought up in the South, and accepting the reality of the situation, Ali stayed on the bus, but egged Bundini on to test the local determination to uphold its laws.

A cautious calm had settled over the arena by fight time. None of the expected fireworks erupted. The prefight ceremonies went off without a hitch. Liston looked stale. He seemed listless, apathetic. He had not handled the long layoff well.

Ali looked sleek and confident. He was all in white, and he seemed ready to rumble, but not hyperexcitable as he had been the first time. Maybe he sensed that this time was going to be easier. The monkey was on Liston's back. Liston had something to prove, not Ali. Liston had quit, not Ali.

The bell sounded and Ali repeated his performance of the first round in the Miami Beach fight. He circled, fleet of foot, shooting out a light jab, with Liston in hot pursuit.

People were still filing in, the cornermen were still arguing about where each of them would sit, and the journalists were still yelling at the photographers to get down, when Liston hit the canvas.

Almost as one, everyone asked, "What happened?"

What happened was that Ali had laid a bear trap and caught a bear. Ali had a deceptive move wherein he threw a jab and bounced into the ropes. As Liston followed with *his* jab, Ali crossed over with a short, stinging right hand. I'd seen him do it in the gym many times.

The blow caught the surprised Liston on the side of the head; he was stunned, lost his balance, and fell. He was not *badly* hurt.

There followed a bizarre set of events only understood after one studies the film and puts a stopwatch on the frame. Let us break down the sequence, bearing in mind that all these events revolved around Ali's luck.

To begin with, there was the question of the referee, in this case the ex-champion Jersey Joe Walcott. It was not unusual to invite a celebrity boxer to referee, but it was ill advised, and the principal cause of the foul-up that took place.

Liston was rolling around the floor like a beached whale. Ali was

The one-round KO in the second Liston fight, May 1965, Lewiston, Maine. *Photo courtesy AP/Wide World Photos*

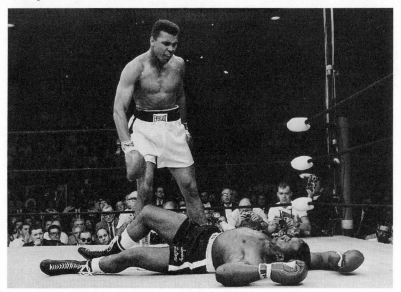

Liston flat on his back. *Photo courtesy AP/Wide World Photos*

standing over him, motioning to him and yelling, "Get up, you bum! No one is going to believe this!"

Walcott did not start the count, but tried to get Ali to a neutral corner, which was the right thing to do. Remember the Dempsey-Tunney long count?

Liston would not get up as long as Ali hovered nearby, waiting to smash him down. Walcott looked bewildered and indecisive.

Now occurred one of those comic moments out of a Mel Brooks movie. A little, wrinkled old man came out of the *audience*, stating that Liston had been down seventeen seconds and that the fight was over. Meanwhile, taking advantage of the confusion over the old man, Liston had gotten up, and *was fighting again.*

The old man was Nat Fleischer, a noted boxing historian, and a respected authority. He was all that, but he *wasn't* a ring official in this fight, so his opinion was just that—an opinion.

Walcott signals that the fight is over. Liston is crestfallen, done in by Ali's luck once again! Ali is jubilant, and those in the press section are in shock, doubting what they have just seen.

Afterward, Ali is shown the replay of what is being referred to as the "Phantom Punch." He watches intently, commenting in his rapid-fire delivery, and suddenly Liston goes down. Ali, himself, having just watched the sequence of blows in *slow motion*, has missed the punch.

"I'm so fast, even I missed the punch on TV."

Pure Ali.

Undaunted, head held high, Muhammad Ali leaves the ring, and his biggest nemesis is *history.*

Epilogue

Sonny Liston did not go quietly into the night, but surfaced in front of the California Boxing Commission to apply for a license to box in that state. When asked why he did not get up if he was not hurt, he answered:

"Commissioner, Muhammad Ali is a crazy man. You can't tell what a crazy man is going to do. He was standing over me, Jersey Joe couldn't control him, and if I got up, I got to put one glove on the canvas to push myself up, and as soon as my knee clears the

Ali, Rahaman, and the author in postfight interview. *Photo courtesy Luisita Pacheco*

canvas Ali is going to be beating on me. The man is crazy, and I figured I ain't getting up till someone controls him."

Remember Ali's explanation of his prefight weigh-in shenanigans? Why was his pressure so high? Why had he gone out of his way to look crazy?

To make Sonny Liston think he *was* crazy. To spook him. To frighten him.

Ali had won both fights at the weigh-in.

Sonny Liston continued to box, fighting sixteen more bouts, but losing his seventeenth to drugs. On January 5, 1971, his wife Geraldine found him dead of an overdose of heroin.

When all evidence is reviewed, scrutinized, and analyzed, the only conclusion we can safely reach is:

Sonny Liston was a victim of *Ali's luck*.

Chapter 11

The Exile Years

From 1968 to October 19, 1970, Muhammad Ali went into involuntary exile due to his refusal to serve in the army. In retrospect, those three years were very important in developing the persona of Ali. Forced to rely on his own initiative and intelligence, shorn of the "support" systems of a superstar, Ali matured into manhood. He grew out of the pampered, protected man-child into a self-confident, rugged individualist, ready to find his own way, unwilling to yield to public opinion, or even to the dictates of his own government. Ali's act took on a different look. He was now approaching martyrdom, and was strong as long as he had the backing and support of his leader, the Honorable Elijah Muhammad. Then, as if Ali were not suffering enough, came a new trial; the Honorable Elijah banished him from his religion.

"I want the world to know that Muhammad Ali has stepped down off the spiritual platform of Islam. . . . We, the Muslims, are not with Muhammad Ali in the desire to work in the sport for the sake of a 'leetle' money. We shall call him Cassius Clay. We take away the name of Allah from him until he proves himself worthy of that name."

Ali took this thunderbolt with his characteristic equanimity and wit. He said, "My daddy is spanking me," and he went on, as he usually did, doing exactly what he was doing before his excommunication. And he continued to be billed as Muhammad Ali, not Cassius Clay.

Ali was faced with the task of supporting his family, and his principal occupation had been denied him. His fallback occupation was cashing in on his celebrity and his ability to speak. This, and the help of many friends, got Ali and his family through the lean years.

It's a tribute to the depth of Ali's loyalty to and faith in the Muslim religion that in the midst of his darkest hour he did not become bitter at being excommunicated. Instead of asking, "Why hath thou forsaken me?" he assumed a cheerful attitude, which was Ali's way. He heard Elijah, but he acted "as if," for Ali knew that if he ever got to be the heavyweight champion, and the millions of dollars started to flow again, he would be welcomed back to the mosque, he would again merit the name Muhammad Ali, a title meaning "worthy of respect" and "beloved of Allah." But for now, an outcast, he would not be abided by the Muslims, and he could not use his Muslim name.

It was during this period that fans came to his aid, and became friends, and stayed with Ali when the good times came back and the Ali Circus began to roll again. One such man was Gene Kilroy, a white entrepreneur and facilitator from Philadelphia. A good high school football player, Kilroy had served as an army officer, and had bounced from job to job, including stints with the Philadelphia Eagles and other NFL teams. He was a crafty Irish go-getter, and he loved Ali and felt bad about how the fighter was being treated. During Ali's exile, Kilroy helped keep him afloat, and while he could be combative and zealous in guarding his position with Ali, Kilroy literally put food on the fighter's table when things got tough. When Ali made it back, he saw to it that Kilroy remained at his side. While he and the Muslims would not publicly acknowledge Kilroy's staunch service during the exile, Ali, by his actions, silently paid Kilroy his due.

But where was the support system? The Muslims, who had made a nice buck with Ali, abandoned him when the Honorable Elijah disowned him. I am certain that many a Muslim on his own slipped Ali some cash, but official aid, in the form of hard currency, was not forthcoming when he needed it most. It is refreshing to note that none of these affronts lessened Ali's affection for the Honorable Elijah or dimmed his fierce belief in the Muslim teachings. Most amazing of all, Ali still does not have a scintilla of bitterness about those days. He became a man. He looks on those days with the eyes of one who notices only positive things and ignores the negative.

It is interesting to note that when Ali was finally allowed to fight, in Atlanta in 1970, the Muslims conveniently forgot that Ali had been banned and joyfully hopped aboard the Ali Circus money-wagon. I don't remember ever hearing of an official edict giving back to Ali the right to use his Muslim name.

By the way, what *was* the offence that caused the Honorable Elijah to expel Ali? It was not that he wanted to fight, but rather that he admitted he needed money. Allah was supposed to take care of that, if you just had *faith*. The Honorable Elijah spoke in these terms: "You tell it, dear apostle. White people wanted Liston to beat up and kill poor little Clay. But Allah and myself said no. This assured his victory."

Perhaps, if one is willing to stretch a point, Allah did look after Ali. Allah gave him Gene Kilroy and friends of his kind, got him speaking engagements, took care of his family in an honorable manner, and, finally, got him a favorable Supreme Court decision and another chance to fight to regain his title. Yes, the Lord Allah works in mysterious ways, if you just *believe*, and Ali believed.

What happened to Herbert Muhammad, Ali's manager and son of the Honorable Elijah? Torn between a fear of his father and his genuine love for Ali, Herbert was in a terrible quandary. For hanging around Ali while the latter was appearing on Broadway in *Buck White*, Herbert was also suspended. Even the faithful brother Rudy had not been around Ali since his suspension, making Herbert's show of love for Ali and disrespect for his father's orders all the more dramatic. When was the suspension lifted? Only Allah knows, but when the smoke cleared in Atlanta, Herbert was still Ali's manager, and so he has stayed to the present day.

In Miami, an inventive broadcast executive named Murray Woroner, who had been re-creating historical events on radio, hit on the idea of creating on a film a computer fight between the only two undefeated heavyweight champions in history: Rocky Marciano and Muhammad Ali.

An ingenious piece of imaginative fluff, it was well scripted, using a panel of experts to feed information into a computer, then carefully filmed in a studio in Miami.

The filming was a great, fun-filled time. Ali, glad to have work to do, and an admiring fan of Rocky Marciano, came to it in high spirits. After all, he was in good hands: Chris Dundee was the referee, Angelo was his cornerman, and I was the doctor at the event.

Rocky was a proud man, but he was in his early forties and his midsection had turned to flab. When he signed to do this fight he asked for time to get in shape, and when he arrived on the set we were amazed to see a rock-hard, trim-fighting-weight, undefeated champion, sporting a new toupee that made him look younger.

The reverse was true of Ali. He was young, and kept himself in reasonable shape, except that his sweet tooth had thickened his midsection. The net effect was that Rocky Marciano looked younger than he was, and Ali looked older.

There were more surprises in store during the shoot. Whereas Ali took all this as a joke, a fantasy, Marciano took it seriously, debating a script point here, an unflattering scene there, and once in a while forgetting himself in the heat of the action and throwing real bombs at Ali's ribs. At one point, Ali went down on one knee after a body shot and we had to call time. Ali hadn't been expecting the blow; Rocky had unwittingly sucker-punched him, and felt bad about it. Still, Ali kept his good humor, dazzled us with his speed and accuracy, coming oh so close with shots, missing by a millimeter. Marciano would always walk away from a round muttering, "My God, the kid is so fast."

The film, when seen today, is a curiosity, but it does have its merits. How does it end? Who wins?

Well, it depends on where the film is shown. In some parts of America, it's Marciano by decision. In other parts, it's Ali by split decision. In England, Ali stops him on cuts. In no part of the universe do Ali or Marciano lose by knockout.

I said it was fiction, but I didn't say it was science fiction.

Woroner was so taken by Ali that he wanted to reinvest his profits and get Ali a license to fight in Florida. This was possible through a connection I had, and a plot was hatched to have a three-fight contract involving Jimmy Ellis (then WBA champion), Joe Frazier, and Ali. It was to be done in the privacy of a television studio and beamed out to pay-per-view customers. Sounded fine, but it was impractical, because the good-hearted Woroner did not understand how the pie was cut up in boxing. Not including the big boys cost him any possibility of accomplishing this ambitious task.

Meanwhile, Ali had been adopted by another white man, Broadway producer Zev Bufman, and had starred in the previously noted play *Buck White*, which opened and closed faster than the Sonny Liston fight. Bufman had found out what we all knew: Ali acts in his own play on a daily basis. But while he's great playing Ali, he's dismal playing anyone else.

Time seemed to be running out on Ali, but he was serenely confident that it would all work out.

There appeared a possibility of a British fight, and Ali met in New York with Jarvis Astaire, the gentleman promoter from London, and boxing manager Mickey Duff. They were riding down Broadway in a limo when Jarvis questioned whether Ali was still an attraction. "How much money you got in your pocket?" Ali asked him.

Jarvis guessed a few hundred.

"I'll bet you I can walk down Broadway for one block, not look at anyone or say anything, and by the end of the block draw a crowd."

So they stopped the limo and Ali started to walk. He was dressed in his usual outfit—black shirt and pants. He walked at a steady pace, looking neither left nor right, not responding to the murmurs of "Ali, Ali," which soon grew to yells. By the end of his walk the crowd was so large that it was blocking traffic. Ali stopped, smiled, waved, stepped back into the limo, and collected his bet.

The oddity was that Ali's luck had held during his exile. "The times they are achangin' . . ." went the hippie anthem of the day, and Ali's image was a heroic one to the rebellious youths who refused to go to Vietnam. "What's Going On?" sang Marvin Gaye, and the most sensible man in the midst of this confusion seemed to be Muhammad Ali. He knew what was going on, man, he knew from the git-go: *Don't go.*

"Those Vietcong ain't done nothin' to me," said Ali, and now, most of the young agreed. Welcome back, Ali the hero. Welcome back from exile, and here, we got a present for you: You can fight Jerry Quarry in Georgia.

The Road Back

Atlanta had not seen such a strange gathering of people since General Sherman had marched his bummers down Peachtree Street and left Atlanta in flames. The veterans of the Ali Circus began to assemble in the best hotel in downtown Atlanta, and the citizens stared in wonderment at the displays of bizarre clothing and recently obtained wealth. A happening of huge proportions was being observed by the people of Atlanta. Not since Clark Gable and Vivien Leigh had come for the premiere of *Gone With the Wind* had so large a crowd been seen.

Ali came back against Jerry Quarry on October 26, 1970, and stopped him on cuts in the third round. Ali looked rusty and his timing was off, but he had taken on a top contender and won.

Ali's luck worked overtime in Atlanta. The camp was set up in a politician's summer quarters, secluded in a wooded glade. Rumors were flying that the "crackers" were out to *get* Ali, and hate letters piled up in the mailbox. Ali was unruffled.

"That ain't my worry. The police got to worry about that."

On several nights, as Bundini and Ali were out taking the cool air, they heard the distant pop of a firearm. Next day, they found bullet holes in the house. This occurred several times, but the distance and the dark made it difficult to say if the riflemen were actually *aiming* at the men or just getting off warning shots. In either case, somebody was shooting at them. You can die just as well from a warning shot as from a bullet intended to hit its target.

Bundini blanched; Ali did not. It did not stop him from strolling after supper, but it made the rest of us edgy and apprehensive.

Knocking out Oscar Bonavena in New York City, December 1970. *Photo courtesy AP/Wide World Photos*

Bundini was so nervous he forgot to bring the protector cup to the stadium on the night of the fight, so Ali had to settle for wearing Rahaman's. It was *that* kind of night.

The Ali Circus moved rapidly to New York in December to fight an Argentine bull named Oscar Bonavena, who had recently given Smokin' Joe Frazier a tough fifteen rounds of hell before losing.

Ali was still rusty. His strength had not returned. Three years of the dietary outrages to which he had subjected his body had made his muscles soft. It figured to be a tough fight, and it was— until the fifteenth, when Ali dropped Bonavena so many times the Argentine began to look like a yo-yo.

Madison Square Garden filled to the rafters with the faithful. Outside of a rock concert, the old Garden had never seen such a collection of garishly dressed people. Old fight fans gawked at the colorful clothes, the displays of wealth, the new kind of fan: the Ali Circus camp followers.

Chapter 12

The Fight: Ali-Frazier I

There were some of us who felt that signing for a March fight with the young, tough Joe Frazier was a mistake. I felt that Ali's body had not achieved the hardness of the preexile years. Some things might never be as they had been. Ali was not as fast, for example, and he could not "dance all night long."

A new Ali emerged from exile. This Ali did not—perhaps, *could* not—float like a butterfly. His "quickness" was not what it had been. Still, if his foot speed was less, his hand speed was not; his hands were still lightning fast.

Ali had always been careful about getting hit, and did not really know if he could take it. Banks had dropped him and Cooper had virtually knocked him out, so he had a basis for doubt. The Bonavena fight had forced him into an unwanted test. Could he take a punch? The answer had come back a resounding "yes." He knew that with Frazier he would have to stand and fight, he would have to take big punches, for his legs would no longer take him effortlessly out of danger. The way Ali trained showed him that he could take body shots. He "gave" the body to his sparring partners (who

95

over the years included future champions Jimmy Ellis, Larry Holmes, and Michael Dokes, all heavy punchers).

Of course, the downside was that he faced serious head injury if he took too many head poundings. But we didn't give much thought to the distant future. We all thought Ali would have a few more fights, then retire. Who could have possibly foreseen the long, tortuous road ahead?

Joe Frazier was a compact, well-muscled heavyweight out of Philly, well managed by crafty Yank Durham. Joe had obliterated Angelo Dundee's new heavyweight champion Jimmy Ellis in 1970 in the Garden in New York.

Joe was an excellent fighter, and much feared because of his drive and aggressive rough-tough style. A small man, he came in low, bobbing and weaving and throwing thunderous hooks to the

Ali and Joe Frazier engage in a shouting match in Madison Square Garden prior to signing for their March 1970 fight. Frazier won the decision and the title. *Photo courtesy UPI/Bettmann*

body that often turned into knockout hooks to the head. He was undefeated, as was Ali, and the fight was so hot it sold itself.

The fight was put together by two unlikely men. Jerry Perenchio was a street guy with a big background in show business, and he was considered a man's man. Jack Kent Cooke, the millionaire owner of big sports franchises, including the Washington Redskins, was considered regal. Maybe "imperious" is a better word. "Distant" also fits.

The Fifth Street Gym came to resemble a vaudeville house. The crowds began to arrive early, and would sit through all the workouts of the lesser fighters, patiently waiting the arrival of Ali and the growing-by-the-day entourage. Leroy Neiman, the famous painter of sports scenes, was present daily. Gordon Parks, the film producer-director, author, and photographer, was sent by *Life* magazine to do a cover and produced the definitive picture of Ali training in his prime.

Don Dunphy, who was going to do the blow-by-blow, brought

The author with the artist, Leroy Neiman, "the best recorder of the boxing scene since George Bellows." *Photo courtesy Luisita Pacheco*

Burt Lancaster, who was going to do the analysis, to the gym, but they went virtually unnoticed. Ali was the star of the Fifth Street Gym. Author Budd Schulberg also was a daily visitor. Many other important writers from America and abroad showed up at the Fifth Street Gym as well.

Amidst this pandemonium, a continuous warfare started up between the Muslims, who had their journalist, Richard Durham ("Hemingway" was his nickname inside the Ali Circus), doing a documentary, and Perenchio's TV/film crew, who were attempting the same thing. Battles flared daily, and Ali watched with his bemused smile, adding just the right touch of kerosene to the fire when things quieted down.

One scene remains in my mind. As Ali lay on his training table

The author with the conditioner, Louis Sarria, and the novelist Budd Schulberg in the 5th Street Gym in Miami Beach. *Photo courtesy Kurt Severin*

after a long sparring session, Durham on one side yelled at Perenchio on the other, "This ain't no plantation deal! You don't get the house, the field hands, and all the cotton for no two and a half million!"

Perenchio gritted his teeth. He was, after all, one of the toughest negotiators in Hollywood. Pointing a manicured fingernail at Ali's sweaty chest, he said, "We got a contract for this." Perenchio did not say "for Ali," but "for this," as if Ali were a chunk of meat or a piece of furniture he was haggling over.

The battles sputtered and sparked on, and through it all Ali smiled his seraphic smile. He was in his element. This was his place, his time, his people. He loved the action, the hustle, the bustle of a big-fight training camp.

Joe Frazier, on the other hand, was strictly a blue-collar, coal-mining, hard and heavy trainer. He spouted no poetry, made no predictions, called no rounds, claimed no movie stars as friends. His camp was all business, and the inhuman training he put himself through was fueled by hatred. Joe Frazier never understood that he was part of the Act, that he was a costar, if a lesser one. For one fight, Joe Frazier became white, the public made him the good guy, the white guy, who was going to shut up the Black Muslim, draft-dodging, unpatriotic, loudmouth nigger, Muhammad Ali. In his rage, Frazier did not pay attention to all the fancy writer's talk of becoming a white hope. Joe was Joe . . . a decent, hardworking, talented, tough fighting machine in his prime. He resented Ali being treated like a champ, and he resented Ali's star billing, and he resented Ali's act. He was a fighter, pure and simple. He sneered at Ali appearing on "The Johnny Carson Show," Ali being all over the papers, Ali showing up on radio and TV.

In Philly, Smokin' Joe Frazier trained for what he knew would be an epic battle. A battle of endurance. A battle of skill, a battle of attrition, and finally a battle of willpower. If Frazier lost this battle it would be because they carried him out on a stretcher. If he was standing at the fifteenth, he figured, he would be a winner. Of all Ali's opponents, I have never seen a more determined man answer the opening bell than Joe Frazier on that March night in Madison Square Garden.

If ever there was a prefight hoopla to match the one for this bout, I would like to know of it. It seemed as if all of Harlem was in the Garden that night, dressed to kill and loving every moment of the excitement. They mingled with the hoity-toity of New York society, stars of the theater, movies, and TV, Washington politicians, men of Wall Street, pimps, hustlers, sportsmen, and crime figures.

In the dressing room area, battles were still flaring between management and the Ali entourage. Bundini had invited about forty friends, and he was outside the building being refused admission for them. The problem was that without the streetwise, irrepressible Bundini, there would be no fight. Madison Square Garden consultant Harry Markson was clearly no match for Bundini. In high dudgeon, Markson came into Ali's dressing room and explained the problem to the smiling fighter. Ali shrugged.

"Well, if I was you, I'd let them in."

"But, there's not a seat in the house. . . . The fire laws prevent us from letting forty people in without seats. . . ."

"If I was you, I'd let them in," repeated Ali, indicating that the subject was closed. Poor Markson: the victim of Ali madness. He went sputtering into the hall, indicating to the guard that Bundini and his forty friends should be permitted entrance.

It was just one of many crazy incidents that characterized the weeks before "The Fight." Ali loved it, drew strength from it. Frazier ignored it and concentrated on coming into the ring in the best condition of his life. With Yank Durham and the clever Eddie Futch, Frazier knew he had the plan to beat Ali. Now, all he had to do was implement that plan.

The Fight

Ali came in resplendent in a red robe with white trim, his cornermen in new red sweaters with MUHAMMAD ALI on the back in white letters. Angelo, though not a superstitious man, always wore the same white sweater for every fight. Since he had many fighters, there was no writing on the back of it. I saw his face when he was told he'd have to wear the red sweater. He looked fear-stricken, but Angelo is a man who doesn't make waves or put negative thoughts in his fighter's head, so he grudgingly wore it. In view of the outcome of the fight, perhaps Angelo's fear was well founded.

Something else bothered me. My wife, Luisita, comes from a family with claims to psychic powers. They are descendants of the Plains Indians, mixed with Spanish blood, and many is the dream that comes true. Right before the fight, Luisita, who was new to the world of boxing, told me that Ali was going to lose. She described having seen the dream as through a telescope. She saw the ring and the crowd around it. She saw Ali, dressed in red trunks with white stripes. She saw him fall to the canvas, his feet in the air, the tassels dancing crazily around his white shoes, and Frazier looking down at him. She saw the crowd stunned. Then she woke up.

I am a scientifically trained man who believes what he can prove, but I leave a tiny corner of belief for things that cannot be proven. I did not know what that dream meant; I only knew it was not a good sign.

Frazier came in wearing green trunks with yellow trim. He stayed in his corner, looking grimly purposeful. Ali danced around the ring in ever-enlarging circles, finally almost brushing up against Frazier. The crowd went crazy. They loved it. Frazier did not.

The stage was set for what was to be a memorable night. The electricity in the Garden before the opening bell was static. The eclectic crowd leaned forward in their seats. The roar was inhuman. It was a primal scream of anticipation. I've never again heard such a sound. It was the opening of a great drama, an epic battle between two undefeated champions in their prime.

Rounds one to four saw Ali mount a serious attack in an effort to knock out Frazier if possible, and if not, to put so much "hurt" on Smokin' Joe that it would discourage him from launching his all-out assault on Ali's body.

Ali found out in the first round that contrary to what he had seen in the films, Joe Frazier was difficult to hit with the jab. Ali had the finest jab in the heavyweight division since Joe Louis's paralyzing hand. The jab controlled the fight; it took the opponent out of his game plan and made him adjust to Ali's, and as soon as that happened it automatically gave Ali the advantage of being able to dictate the pace and tempo of the fight.

Simply put, Frazier understood that his face would lump up, be cut and bruised, and that his eyes would close up, but he was willing to give Ali that advantage, because the trade-off was that it would be *Frazier* dictating the pace and tempo. Frazier would decide where and when to fight. By round four, it was evident that Frazier's plan was to fight while pinning Ali on the ropes. His pace would be all-out, and his main tactic would be nonstop pressure — relentless, unforgiving, punishing pressure. By the end of four, with Ali comfortably ahead on the scorecards, Ali had landed his best shots and Frazier had just smiled and moved forward. Frazier was a tank churning forward in spite of antitank shells bouncing off the turret.

In the fourth came a golden moment for Ali. He landed a powerful combination. Frazier staggered, and Ali supporters were on their feet yelling hysterically, but the gritty Frazier shook it off and came back to the attack. Visions of King Kong atop the Empire State Building deflecting the bullets of the attacking biplanes raced through my mind. I glanced at Budd Schulberg, who was huddled in our corner. He looked worried. Bundini was hysterical, yelling unintelligible exhortations at Ali, and Angelo was grim. Round four, with eleven rounds to go!

The sixth opened with Frazier taunting Ali and driving him into the ropes, where Frazier set up shop and started to whittle down Ali with devastating hooks to his hip joints. As in a later fight with Frazier, Ali began to develop blood blisters (hematomas), and the effect of blood in the hip joint is both painful and debilitating. Joe was starting to shoot out Ali's tires. Ali was definitely not "floating like a butterfly."

Frazier was living up to his prefight strategy: Pressure. Pressure. "Sooner or later Ali's got to stop and fight. Then I got him," Frazier had said.

From round one to round five, Ali had stood in his corner between rounds, refusing to sit down and rest. He was trying to psych Frazier, but Frazier had sat and rested and had refused to even notice that Ali was standing. From round six on, Ali sat. No fool,

Ali. When he saw Frazier wasn't going for his jive, he sensibly abandoned the ploy.

Ali always outtalked any opponent. On this night, Frazier talked so much that referee Arthur Mercante spent the night telling both men to shut up. The action was so fast and furious that Don Dunphy, the blow-by-blow telecaster, said, "Mercante is telling both men to stop talking. When are they finding time to talk?"

When Ali was hit by a particularly hard shot, he would grab Frazier behind the head and pull him in to his chest. Since he was much taller, this would leave Ali with his head sticking out above Frazier. At this point, Ali would shake his head at the crowd, disclaiming the effectiveness of the punch, and he would yell at the huge press section, "Nooooooo contest!"

The crowd loved the clowning; the judges didn't; and more important, Joe Frazier didn't pay it any attention, and when Mercante would break them, admonishing Ali over and over again not to pull Frazier by the head, Joe would again launch his battering-ram approach to Ali's body. "How much more of this can Ali take?" we thought in the corner. "Get off the ropes, Ali," Angelo yelled over and over, his voice getting more strident with each round.

Eddie Futch, the genial, modest strategist in Frazier's corner, wanted to have Joe take advantage of one of his disadvantages. Joe was considerably shorter, so Eddie had him bob and weave to make himself even shorter, in order to rob Ali of his jab. When Frazier started to fight straight up, he was pummeled by Ali. When I asked Futch why his fighter straightened, he answered, "Doc, it is exhausting to bob and weave for fifteen rounds. You gotta take a break." So even Frazier was getting tired. Even Smokin' Joe was human! The pace was starting to tell on both men.

Frazier's pressure was clearly winning the fight for him in rounds seven through ten. Frazier was fighting his fight. He was in command; he dictated when and where to fight. Frazier was paying a terrible price, to be sure. One does not come down the road to Ali's body without paying a high toll. Frazier's face was falling apart. Blood stained his mouthpiece and his eyes were closing, but still, undaunted, he pressed forward, landing his sledgehammer blows to the body of the rapidly sagging Ali. Ali began to commit uncharacteristic errors. He was hooking with the best left hooker in boxing, a sure prescription for unconsciousness. Again and again, Frazier got the best of these hook-for-hook exchanges. By round ten Eddie Futch had spotted a possibly fatal flaw in Ali's offense. As Ali uppercut with his right hand, he left that side of his face open to a sweeping left hook, Joe's best punch. Again and again, Joe tried the hook as he saw Ali shoot out an uppercut. Frazier was landing, although not with the force he wanted. Not *yet*, anyway.

And so the eleventh started with the same pas de deux, and with the thought in my head that Ali had won the ten-round fight, but was losing the fifteen-rounder. The Championship Causeway is from rounds eleven to fifteen, it is in these painful rounds that the championship is won or lost. Fatigue is your enemy. The accumulation of blows begins to tell. Frazier's face was falling apart, but Ali's legs were turning to stone. Desire and willpower, the absolute refusal to accept defeat, the ability to summon up some extra strength, to tap an unknown reservoir—all these are factors in deciding whether victory or defeat will be a fighter's fate.

Round eleven—"the Gruesome Eleventh," as we called it, or "the Long Walk," as Frazier's corner dubbed it—was the turning point of the fight. There are rounds that pinpoint the exact time a fight was won or lost. The eleventh was such a round in this fight. After the eleventh Ali would need a miracle to win, and miracles seldom happen inside the square circle. Toward the beginning of the eleventh round, Ali started a hook, but Frazier's hook was faster, stronger, and more accurate. It landed flush on target. Ali's legs buckled. His eyes glazed and he fell to the ropes, with Frazier in snarling pursuit. I looked at the ring clock. Two minutes to go. "We'll never make it!" I thought.

Ali moved on leaden legs, his eyes glazed, sluggishly trying to keep Frazier away with ineffectual punches, looking doomed. But what a man does in a moment of imminent defeat is sometimes more meaningful in evaluating his persona than what he does to win. It was now that Ali proved to the world that he was no mere pretty boy, no soft pushover. Now, he "shocked and amazed" the world so it could see what a few of us already knew. Beneath that baby-face mask was the countenance of a warrior—as tough as the ugliest, most scarred, flat-nosed, cauliflower-eared pug.

Ali reeled around the ring, trying to do what he had done to Liston, extending his long left, holding Frazier away by stiff-arming his head. With ten seconds to go, Ali was out on his feet, and he tottered back across the ring on jelly legs. One simple punch by Frazier would have knocked him out, but Frazier, falling victim to the Ali act, held off, fearing a trap. It worked, and Ali survived the round. Angelo met him halfway to the corner with a spongeful of cold water. Ali looked blank-eyed as Bundini cried and quietly went about his work of reviving him, of feeding him simple commands. Ali perked up. The worst was over. If he could survive the Gruesome Eleventh, he could withstand any assault.

The twelfth round saw Ali regain his strength and fight off suddenly cautious Frazier. Was Frazier showing Ali too much respect? Yank Durham had said to Frazier, "Watch out when you hurt Ali— a man is most dangerous when he is hurt." Perhaps Frazier had listened too closely to his mentor. Unbelievably, considering the battering Ali had taken in the eleventh, Ali won the twelfth round, but I was shocked to see a huge bulge on the side of his face. Was his jaw broken? It sure looked that way, but there was no complaint of pain from Ali. Still, the jaw was very swollen.

Ali spent the thirteenth round leaning on the turnbuckles of a neutral corner. Frazier set about his deadly work, pummeling him. Bundini would yell, over and over, as if in a hypnotic state, "God's in your corner!" Not in the thirteenth he wasn't.

Round fourteen saw Frazier grinning, reveling in the joy of combat, his face contorted by abrasions, hematomas, and contusions. Saliva drooled from his swollen lips, and he was breathing in gasps. Frazier was snorting through his nose, which forces air into the sinuses, and this contributed to the swelling in his face. Ali was coolly boxing, still talking to the press and giving the impression that he thought he was winning the fight. Ali's act. It had always worked before. Joe looked arm-weary but still doggedly determined. The Garden's Harry Markson likened Joe Frazier to a pit bull on the attack. Ali managed to win the round by a narrow margin. The fight was still up for grabs.

So, as it sometimes happens, it came down to the fifteenth round. The hell of the previous fourteen rounds was meaningless; the winner of the fifteenth would win the fight.

At this point Eddie Futch's insightful analysis of a basic Ali flaw came into play. As Ali started a right uppercut, Frazier threw an all-or-nothing left hook. It landed flush on Ali's exposed jaw, and Ali fell on his back, his feet flying in the air, tassels dancing—just as Luisita had seen it.

The Garden is on its feet roaring. The foxy ladies are crying into their minks; the men stand with mouths ajar. Ali down? It can't be!

"Get up, Champ," they yell until they are hoarse, and then I find that I, too, am yelling. Schulberg looks lost. Angelo is halfway up the ring stairs, towel in hand. Bundini is yelling at the top of his voice.

Frazier's corner is yelling its own instructions to a weary Smokin' Joe, who is standing in a neutral corner, praying Ali will stay down—praying this personal hell he finds himself in is at an end, that he has taken his last punch from Ali.

But, no, Ali will not stay down. As long as he is conscious, Ali will stand. Ali is up, eyes cloudy, but awake enough for Mercante to motion the two fighters back into action.

A cheer goes up—or possibly a wail, exclaiming: "Oh God, he's up; *now* he's going to get it."

But the wind seems to have gone out of Frazier's sails. He tries to summon up the overdrive of the previous rounds, but his gas tank is close to empty.

Ali lost the round, lost the fight. No argument there. Afterward, Frazier, his face a mask of pain, eyes closing, holding ice bags to his jaw, said simply, "That man can sure take punches. I went to the country, back home, for some of the shots I hit him with."

Ali said, "Everyone will remember what happened here. What I want them to remember is my art and my science."

But what we remembered was his courage, his toughness, and his championship heart.

Second Ali-Frazier, January 28, 1974, New York City, N.Y.

This was probably the greatest anticlimax in Ali's long history. Frazier had lost his title to George Foreman in Jamaica in 1973

by knockout. He was trying to fight his way back into title conten-
tion. Ali had gone on to win nine fights, but had lost to Ken Norton
in the broken-jaw fight (more on that later). The money fight appeared to be Ali-Foreman, since no one gave Frazier any chance
in a rematch with huge, powerful George Foreman. So, the second
Ali-Frazier was a sort of elimination bout for a title shot with
Foreman.

It was not even a dull replay of the first epic encounter; nor
could anyone have predicted the magnitude of the third encounter
off this anticlimactic second fight.

Ali beat Frazier easily, because he was able to do what he had
not been able to in the first fight. He controlled Frazier with his
jab, and if Frazier came too close, Ali grabbed the back of his head
and pulled him in and smothered him. Frazier lacked his old fire.
The Foreman domination had sapped his confidence. Oh, he tried,
but his animal intensity was not there. Nor was the crowd's. Miracles seldom happen twice in one spot. The fans sold out the Gar-

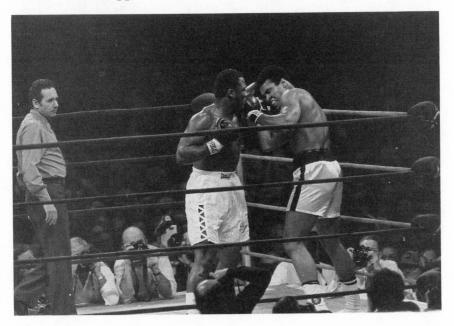

Ali and Frazier at the Garden in January 1974. *Photo courtesy AP/Wide
World Photos*

den, but there was no sense of occasion, no sense of seeing a great event. It was more like revisiting a battlefield, one on which two ex-champions, edging into retirement, were meeting to pick up a nice paycheck.

For the record, Ali won the fight. Probably he won too handily, for when it came time to give Frazier a third fight, Ali remembered this second one, remembered Frazier as a somewhat shot fighter, and allowed himself to get trapped in that grim battle of attrition that came to be known as the "Thrilla in Manila."

Chapter 13

The Tough Nut:
Ali-Norton

Following his dramatic loss to Joe Frazier, Ali launched on a busy
schedule of exhibitions (twenty-eight in all) and fights (he won all
six) and was working his way toward a lucrative rematch with Joe
Frazier when he took an "easy" fight with a young ex-Marine, Ken
Norton of San Diego.

Norton had the physique of a Greek god, and was trained by
the master of ring strategy, Eddie Futch. Norton had an awkward
style, a cross between the shuffling, drag-a-foot-behind-you style
of Quasimodo, the Hunchback of Notre Dame, and the crossed-
arm bob and weave of Archie Moore. Norton was hard to hit, and
he could punch.

Ali's luck was about to fail him.

The entire training period was a joke. The Ali Circus had been
going from fight to fight, exhibition to exhibition, at high speed.
Ali fought light heavyweight champion Bob Foster in Nevada, then
Joe Bugner in Vegas, and had fought seventeen exhibitions in the

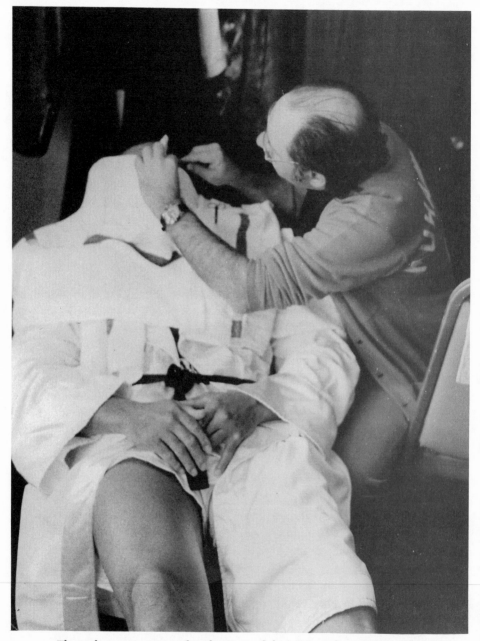

The author sewing a cut after the Foster fight in November 1972, Stateline, Nevada. It was the only time Ali was cut. *Photo courtesy Luisita Pacheco*

year prior to the Ken Norton fight in San Diego. Is there any wonder that Ali considered the nonstop action as a continuous period of training? His dismissal of this fight as just another pit stop on his run for the heavyweight championship would cost him dearly. Ken Norton was not a man to be underestimated.

The fight started with a deceptively slow first round. Ali could not find Norton's head to jab him, and Norton seemed satisfied to land an occasional zinging shot to Ali's jaw.

In the second round, Norton went into high gear. Ali was surprised. Norton seemed to have a game plan for beating Ali, he was in super shape, and he was fighting with all the élan of the Marines storming the beaches at Iwo Jima.

Ali came back to the corner in pain. In his stoical manner he said, "Something's wrong—I can move my jaw with my tongue."

An immediate examination revealed a fractured jaw. Normally it would have been medically mandatory to stop the fight then and there. But Ali would have not accepted the idea that he should quit fighting simply because he was at a disadvantage. In his champion's heart, Ali felt he could beat Norton, and if he couldn't, it wouldn't be because of a broken jaw, it would be because Norton was a better man that day. Even after being told his jaw was broken, Ali emphatically refused to have the fight stopped.

As a ghetto doctor, I have been around a lot of pain and suffering, and I understand bravery in the face of adversity. On that hot day in San Diego, I got a new perspective on Ali, the man. I also got a whole truckload of respect for his stoic acceptance of his bad luck, for his ability to handle pain, for his will to carry on, to overcome any desire to quit, to go on uncomplaining, to finish the fight.

Oh, how Ali grew in the boxing fraternity's estimation. Once again, he was out on the end of the limb, sawing away. In losing to Norton, he actually won—he won the respect of his boxing peers. They knew from the Frazier fight that he was tough, from the Norton fight, they learned *how* tough.

To understand the complexities of working with Ali in those days, one must examine the decisions to be made during that bout.

As the doctor in the corner, my vote was to stop the fight immediately. Angelo felt Ali had a shot at stopping Norton, but seeing

A serious prefight interview before the Ali-Norton match in March 1973, when Ali lost in twelve. *Photo courtesy Luisita Pacheco*

that it was not Ali's day, that Norton had Ali's number and was on his way to beating him, Angelo would have preferred to stop it because of the fracture.

But Ali had grown into more than just a boxer in the eyes of black America; he was an authentic folk hero. In addition, white liberals protesting the Vietnam War held Ali in high esteem. To quit when things got tough was not Ali's way, and, worse, it would damage his growing popularity—a factor that figured into any decision-making concerning Ali, who was probably the most ad-mired role model for young blacks struggling to assert their newly won civil rights and to gain confidence in their "blackness."

In the corner of this great champion were two white men with professional obligations that we struggled to separate from racial or political considerations. In any case, I, as the doctor, knew the fight must be stopped to obviate the possibility of further damage that might make the surgery more complicated and the recovery period longer and more arduous. My vote, even considering racial factors, was to stop the fight early.

As for the other white man, Angelo Dundee, Ali's chief second, he was not as aware as I of the racial implications of a white man's stopping a fight, especially against an opponent considered "easy" by the public and the boxing fraternity. Norton was a big betting underdog that day. What makes Angelo Dundee the premier cor-nerman of the day is his ability to focus on a fight and to not be distracted by ancillary matters. Angelo can work through an earth-quake and not notice it if the fight is hot and heavy and important. The other side of that coin is that Angelo feels his fighter cannot be beaten, and, consequently, he is loath to stop a fight while his boxer is breathing.

In the case of Ali, Angelo felt that Ali would pull the fight out at any moment. Ali did not want the fight stopped, and that was all Angelo needed to hear. When it became apparent, even to Angelo, that Ali was losing, then a different problem presented itself—a problem of "position" in the race to the title. Ali did not need a loss to a little-regarded fighter; it would set him back in the ratings. But a stoppage due to a broken jaw would not hurt Ali. It was almost an act of God, an accident, unrelated to boxing skill—in short, a perfect alibi. Now, Angelo was in the same profes-sional quandary as I was.

I felt the fight should be stopped on medical grounds. Angelo could see the saving grace of a TKO on the grounds of an injury. However, Ali's pride was such that he would rather have endured pain, and a defeat by decision, and a fall in the ratings, than have had it recorded that another man had stopped the great Ali—especially a West Coast fighter like Ken Norton. After all, the

record book wouldn't read "Ali TKO'd because of a broken jaw";
it would just say "Ali TKO'd by Norton."

The final say, even above Ali's decision, was up to Herbert Muhammad, the manager. He was most acutely aware of the many
extraneous factors involved in the Ali career. Aside from his im-
portance to the black movement in America, Ali was vital to the
Black Muslim religion. Converts were flocking to it. Famous basketball stars, football heroes, and other prominent sports figures
were changing their religions and their names. Ali was more than
just a fighter to Herbert Muhammad. Entrusted by Elijah Muhammad to care for, preserve, and nourish the legend, Herbert
was in a tough place. His background and education had not prepared him to make these decisions. He could not call Elijah (no
time) and ask what to do. So he did what most indecisive men do:
nothing. Aware of what criticism and ire it would raise with the
black establishment if a white doctor went to the commission doctor and stopped the fight against Ali and Herbert's wishes, I also
did nothing. Used to taking orders from Herbert and Ali, Angelo,
the last guy to want to stop a fight as long as his fighter wanted to
continue, also took the easy road, and did nothing. Ali, the only
one of us in command of his career, did what he always did—he
took the pain and tried like hell to beat Ken Norton over twelve
painful rounds.

Ali lost a close decision in twelve rounds. His pain was excru-
ciating. A jaw fracture is by its very nature painful; imagine being
hit on the jaw by a powerful puncher for ten rounds. My admi-
ration for Ali jumped 100 percent on that hot, painful day.

Ali was taken to a San Diego hospital. There, Dr. William Lun-
deen, the commission doctor, called in Dr. Lancaster, a plastic
surgeon, who wheeled Ali right into the surgical suite. The operation was simple and straightforward. The fracture was reduced,
and Ali's mouth was wired closed. The Mouth That Roared was
finally shut—for a while, anyway.

The surgery completed, Herbert, Angelo, and I waited for Ali
to regain full consciousness. Herbert and Angelo were misty-eyed,
and the three of us choked up as we tried to reassure Ali that
everything would work out. Ali smiled through swollen lips, and

although his jaw was wired shut, he spoke reassuringly to us. *He was trying to make us feel better!*

"Don't worry about this—it ain't nothing. I put people in the hospital, and now Norton put me in the hospital. That's boxing. That's the way it is." Herbert tried to tell him that the press would see this as a fight Ali had lost because of a broken jaw. Ali shook his head.

"No, Norton beat me today. Fair and square. I tried to win, but he was too tough today. Tomorrow, when I get well, I'll go out and whup his ass, but today, Norton was the better man."

It was an endearing trait of Ali's that after a fight he always spoke highly of his adversary, regardless of the outcome of the fight. Never did Ali demean Norton's ability, never did he offer an excuse. There was only the simple, honest statement, "Norton whupped me."

Ali-Norton, September 10, 1973, Los Angeles

As soon as Ali was pronounced fit to box again, he went into intense training to fight a rematch with Ken Norton.

The fight was anticlimactic. Ali gave Norton a boxing lesson, but it still went the distance and ended in a close decision. The fight was held in the L.A. Forum and was almost a repeat of the first fight, but there were some important differences. First, Ali was not fighting with a broken jaw, was not fighting pain as well as Norton. Second, while they each fought the same fight, Ali fought like the *real* Ali, while Norton boxed the same—he had no surprises to spring, no new tricks to show. Norton was Norton, but now, without the injury, and properly trained, Ali was his real self, a superb defensive fighter. Ali outthought and outfought Norton, although the hometown California fans questioned the decision.

Some boxers always gave Ali trouble, and Ken Norton was certainly at the top of that list.

Chapter 14

The Rumble in the Jungle

Of all the fights that Ali had during the worldwide travels of the Ali Circus, the George Foreman fight in Africa was easily the most bizarre.

George Foreman had won a gold medal in the 1968 Olympics, overpowering opposition with his sledgehammer blows, and had gone on to win the title with a decisive battering of Joe Frazier in Jamaica on January 22, 1973. Foreman had since defended the title two times, knocking out both opponents in early rounds. One of them was Ken Norton, who had lasted two rounds before being run over by the Foreman Express. By the time Foreman got around to fighting Ali, he had knocked out both men who had beaten Ali (Frazier and Norton) and had won forty straight fights, thirty-seven of them by knockout. Big George looked unbeatable. Big George was physically impressive, and had a surly, nasty disposition. Does this remind you somewhat of Sonny Liston? It had been ten years since Ali had taken the title from the "unbeatable"

116

Sonny Liston in Miami Beach. Again Ali was the underdog; again it looked like an impossible dream.

It was Don King who had the impossible dream, and it took his considerable genius for wheeling and dealing to create a miracle. Don King was a numbers man from Cleveland who had done time for manslaughter. He and a colleague had disagreed about a mathematical question, and Don had smote the man a mighty blow. Sometime in the moment between his receiving the blow and his head hitting the curb, life left his body. King was sent away, and did his time well. He spent his time reading Shakespeare and the Harvard Classics, and came out of his incarceration a confirmed sesquipedalian. Big words, not fists, were to be his weapons in future disagreements.

The crowd cheering Ali and George Foreman before their October 1974 battle in Kinshasa, Zaire. *Photo courtesy Luisita Pacheco*

I first met Don King when he brought his fighter Earnie Shavers to New York to fight Jimmy Ellis. He was bigger than his fighter, and much more impressive. Don stands six-foot-three and is even taller if one measures his hair, which stands straight up on his head, adding a good three inches to his height. He is dynamic. He has a deep voice that crackles with electricity. He has piercing eyes. He can be ominous, then turn jolly, with a booming laugh and a blinding smile. Blessed with a con man's brain and a revival preacher's rap, King can talk anybody into anything.

On the night that Shavers leveled Ellis in round one, Don was busy getting his foot into Ali's door. He was already a pal of Foreman, having attended George's execution of Joe Frazier. King, a man who is blessed with the ability to laugh at himself, never

A Foreman montage.

tires of telling the story of how he rode to the Foreman-Frazier fight in the champion's limo (Frazier's) and rode back in the champion's limo (Foreman's).

So, Don King worked his way into the Ali Circus while keeping the Foreman connection alive. Now he needed financial backing. It was here that King showed the world what a shrewd manipulator and deal-maker he was.

Somehow, King had hooked up with the representatives of an obscure African nation, Zaire, who were looking for a way to make their obscure country more widely known.

While filming a documentary for NBC in 1990, I had a chance to talk to one of the two men responsible for the "Rumble in the Jungle," as the Ali-Foreman title fight came to be known. Tishim-

A bemused Ali gazes at a tribal warrior at the Zaire airport, welcoming the Ali circus to Africa.

Two publicity pictures of Ali vs. Foreman. *Photos courtesy UPI/Bettmann*

pupu, a minister of publicity in the Mobutu government, told of going to the post office in Washington, D.C., to mail a package to

Zaire. The clerk had never heard of Zaire, but guessed it was in the Sea of Japan. That did it. Tishimpupu and Mandunga Bula, the man closest to President Mobutu Sese Seko, decided to get an attraction that would put Zaire on the map.

Ruling out assassination of the U.S. president as counterproductive, they came to the doorstep of the giant American black man with the stand-up hair.

Remember, Don King was not a promoter at this time, but had just gotten into boxing through managing Earnie Shavers. In light of what King would soon put together, he has to go down as one of the greatest promoters in the history of boxing.

King now went to Foreman to persuade him to fight Ali in Zaire. King told him he had Ali. Foreman wavered. King told him five million good reasons he should sign. Mission accomplished, King scurried to Ali, and had a similar discussion with him. While waiting to sign the two fighters, King had to get the Africans to commit $12 million. Since the profit/loss margin hung by the thin thread of technology then available to beam the fight to the world, he also had to find and negotiate with a production company that could handle this, and come up with a genius to surmount the enormous technical problems.

Don King contracted with John Daly's production company from London, and he found his technical genius, Hank Kaplan, in New York.

Now that the witches' brew was bubbling, King had to convince all parties that *he* was the promotor for this mega-event. If there was ever a man on earth who knew how to use his color to close a deal, Don King was that man.

His pitch was simple, direct, and appealing: a black champion, a black contender, a black referee, a black Third World country, and . . . a black promoter!

Irresistible.

All of us in the Ali camp were in favor of Don King. The black man had always been shut out as a promoter. He could fight, he could train, he could manage, but he couldn't promote. Why not?

So Don King made his entrance onto the stage of Big-Time Boxing as a promoter. Subsequent events have proven our collective judgment correct. Don King became a top promoter, and as

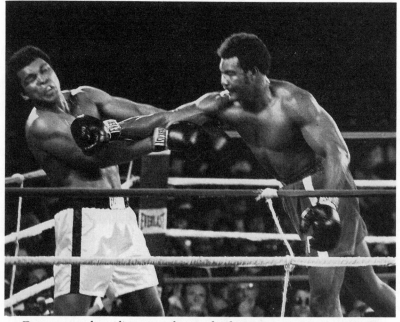

Foreman reaches Ali in an early round. *Photo courtesy UPI/Bettmann*

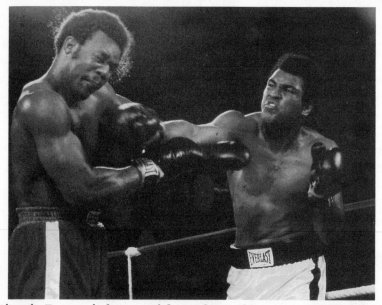

Ali rocks Foreman before an eighth round KO. *Photo courtesy UPI/Bettmann*

ruthless and exploitive as any white promoter ever was. The boxing world is rough, tough, and often brutal—and Don King belongs.

The weeks of training in Zaire passed slowly. Ali was located in the president's compound at N'Zele, forty miles from the bustling capital of Kinshasa. Foreman could not take the quiet of the compound, nor the proximity of Ali, and opted to stay at the Intercontinental Hotel.

From the beginning Ali overwhelmed the Africans with the Act. He was everywhere, and he walked the streets, letting the little people see him, touch him, talk to him. In no time Ali had conquered Zaire.

Foreman, on the other hand, was sullen, surly, withdrawn. He brought over two huge dogs with him. To the Zairians, they were reminders of the days of tough Belgian colonial rule, when the Special Police used dogs on the population. Foreman stayed in his air-conditioned suite, using room service and in general playing the part of the aloof Champion. It did not go down well.

This fight took place at the same time that the black awakening was happening in the United States. Blacks had discovered their roots. "Black is best," said the black leadership, and the crowd roared back, "Black is beautiful."

A wave of blackness swept America. No longer did the black man straighten his hair, no longer did he wear three-button, vested suits, no longer did he try to "whiten up."

It was in this heady spirit of awakening that Don King sold his fight to travel and ticket agents. This would be a black Woodstock.

Then enthusiasm ran headlong into reality. It started when King, ever the publicity man, ran off thousands of posters that said: FROM THE SLAVE SHIP TO THE CHAMPIONSHIP.

The posters were beautiful, but the thought was not. A stern Zaire official banned them.

"We are the winners of that struggle. We sold the slaves and stayed in Africa. You were the slaves and were sent to America."

So much for that good idea.

The American blacks who traveled happily to Zaire went dressed in dashikis, with their hair styled in elaborate bubble Afro do's and their feet wrapped in leather-thong sandals.

Imagine their shock as they hit the streets of Kinshasa and found the population dressed in sneakers and regular clothes from off the rack at K Mart, and sporting close-cropped haircuts. Just like in Cleveland. Imagine their shock as they saw the Africans regard them with disbelief. In Zaire, there was widespread mirth over the getup of the American blacks. It was a deflating experience for them.

And King found that while all Zairians assured him that any thorny issue, technical drawback, or local situation could be handled easily, the quick "No problem, sir" usually translated to "Big Problem." The travel tours got bogged down in red tape and technical hassles that were never resolved. The expected avalanche of American blacks at events never materialized.

King, his heart and mind in the right place, wanted to give the natives a treat. He got top black jazz and rock 'n' roll acts together and gave a concert.

Now, Zairians have to be at work early and do not, as a rule, stay up late. Anyone with even a slight knowledge of rock 'n' roll artists knows that their hearts don't start beating until midnight. Net result: a thin audience, which boded poorly for a 4 A.M. fight.

Those Africans who were present were amazed by the pyrotechnics of James Brown, but were startled by the thin, reedlike voices of the Pointer Sisters, dressed in thirties clothes. The concert was great for the press and for Americans stuck in Zaire, but a distinct washout for Zairians.

Even the concert gave King problems. The hotel tab was astronomical. The room-service bill alone was $150,000! Practical Zairians impounded the musicians' instruments and equipment until the account was settled. King's maneuvering during this time was awesome to behold. He sent emissaries hither and yon—to London, to Liberia—to borrow money against the show's profit. Every day was firing-squad day. Somehow, King overcame his problems—but meanwhile, a bigger problem presented itself.

With the fight days away, with his impossible dream about to come true, King received a near-fatal shock: George Foreman was cut in training.

George Foreman had been increasingly unhappy in his hotel suite at the Intercontinental. The devilish Drew Bundini Brown had infiltrated the hotel staff and was busily spreading rumors that the Ali people were poisoning Foreman's food. George went for that like Charley the Tuna. He had tasters, he had food brought in from America and Europe, he did everything he could to keep from being poisoned. Bundini reported to Ali, and as they had done since the Liston days, they laughed and plotted more mischief.

So it was with great doubt that Ali received the news of the Foreman laceration. Could we see it? No. No one was able to take a close look at it. Was it a ploy to get out of the fight?

Net Result: fight postponed four weeks.

As it turned out, it was just another case of Ali's luck. Ali, now thirty-two and needing time to acclimate, to fine-tune his aging machinery, and beginning to draw spiritual strength from being in Africa, used the time wisely. Foreman, his training restricted because of the cut, unhappy in his hermit existence, and getting more anxious every day, suffered over the delay.

Again we think back to the second Liston fight. Liston had readied his thirtysomething body, and young Ali comes up with a hernia and postpones the fight two months—and is helped by the delay.

Now, the younger man suffers, and the older man benefits. Typical Ali luck.

There were other benefits as well. King and his hardworking technicians had met unthought-of complications. If the fight had gone off on schedule, they might not have been able to beam out a picture.

This would have spelled financial disaster, plus big problems with Mobutu Sese Seko, who was getting testy about the negative publicity his country was receiving. After all, the purpose of the fight was to show everybody that this Third World country could handle big business enterprises and sporting events. Also, Mobutu wanted the world to know where his country was located on the map. Failure now would mean Don King was in Big Trouble.

The delay helped solve problems. A good example of this was the ticket foul-up. The site chosen for the fight was a football stadium. There were no seats, only broad concrete benches upon which folding chairs were placed.

King asked for the seating chart so that he could order the tickets printed in Philadelphia. King was told that he should print up the tickets and that they would then fit the seats according to the tickets. Patently impossible. How many aisles? How many rows? How many seats per row?

In spite of this foul-up, King ordered the tickets. They came on the Tuesday before the fight, which was to be held that Saturday. The Zaire official took one look at them and said, "Send 'em back."

"Why?" asked the incredulous King.

"Because our president's name is spelled wrong."

Back went the tickets. Then Foreman got cut, and King had caught another break—courtesy of Ali's luck.

I arrived in N'Zele after the delay to find that Dr. Charles Williams, Herbert's doctor, had examined Ali and said the cause of his dizziness after a workout was hypoglycemia. Dr. Williams had prescribed a treatment for this, to be given the night of the fight. He would have Lana Shabazz cook up a peach cobbler pie and put a pint of ice cream on it. "If your gas tank is low, you gotta put in more gas," he said with a warm smile.

Hypoglycemia is a condition where the mechanism that produces insulin, which is used to burn off sugar, is producing too much and consequently causing the blood sugar to drop to a dangerously low level. If *more* sugar is ingested, more insulin is pumped out, and so sugar levels are made even lower. In other words, sugar is the *last* thing to give a hypoglycemic.

Hypoglycemia is a diagnosis that can be made only by laboratory analysis, not physical examination. So, suddenly, I had a problem.

How could I tell Herbert's Muslim doctor that he didn't know what he was talking about? Being in the Ali Circus required finesse and diplomacy, so I suggested compromise.

"Look, Doc, Ali can't eat an hour before a fight, because he is going to get hit in the abdomen by the heaviest puncher in the world. He'll throw up in the middle of the ring."

"Oh," he said, faint lights glowing in the darkness of his head.

"So," I said, "I'll make up an orange syrup. Pour syrup into his orange juice bottle and feed it to him, bit by bit, during the fight, so we can keep the tank full."

"Great," he said, relieved to find such an easy solution to such a gigantic problem.

That useless bottle is still out in the jungle, somewhere between N'Zele and the stadium.

Even doctors were now layering in to the Ali Circus. That same doctor followed us to Manila and tried to feed Ali pastries before the fight. Eventually, he was to take over and feed Ali thyroid hormone, amphetamines, and diuretics before the Holmes fight.

Another self-appointed medical expert surfaced in C. B. Atkins, an adviser to Herbert on "business matters." Since the exile, Ali's hands had gotten soft, and they'd get hurt during fights, so I'd started to shoot them with novocaine. C. B. decided on the night of the Foreman fight that Ali's hands shouldn't be numbed.

It took time to convince C. B. that the shots had no effect on the speed of Ali's hands.

Another complication taken care of.

The fight was set for 4:00 A.M. of a hot, humid, Zairian night, with huge rain clouds roiling on the horizon and threatening the sixty thousand fans who had started appearing at six that evening.

Ali and the entourage prepared themselves at 1:00 A.M. and headed for the stadium. The mood was grim. Only Ali laughed and joked.

The long wait, the endless African nights, the mind-boggling complications, the arguments, and the doubts were over. As we entered the stadium, we heard the crowd chant "Ali Boom-ay-yee" ("Ali, kill him") and saw the tribal performers break into their dance. As they say in the old movies, the joint was jumping. Ali broke into his broad grin. This was more like it. This was his crowd. He was in command. Now, all he needed to do was execute, and only he knew how he was going to beat the Mummy, George Foreman.

The Fight

The night before the fight, Foreman had called Mobutu aide Bula to his hotel and informed him that he could not go through with the fight until Joe Bugner, the ranked English heavyweight, signed a contract to fight Foreman after Foreman beat Ali. Bula, his reputation on the line, could not understand what the fighter was saying.

"So, sign when you want, but you must fight Ali tomorrow night."

"Bula, I want to fight Bugner immediately after I beat Ali. On the same night. It will be a record."

Bula respectfully declined to entertain the notion and insisted on the Ali fight, and when Foreman reluctantly agreed, he left, feeling shaken. He went directly to Ali and told him what Foreman had proposed. Ali grinned.

"Now, I know I got George."

As was Angelo Dundee's custom, he went to the stadium that afternoon to check the ring. He found it lopsided. He had to put chocks under one side of the ring to balance it, and the canvas had to be stretched properly. Dundee had Bobby Goodman, a young PR guy, with him, and they found the ring ropes sagging. Taking large screwdrivers, they began turning the buckles, but there was only so much that could be done. The ropes were loose.

The strategy that Ali and Dundee had envisioned was based on the old "float like a butterfly" technique that had proven so effective against Sonny Liston. The resemblances between the Mummy and the Bear were many. Both were big, ponderous men who depended on their heavy punch to neutralize movement and pulverize opponents. Neither handled fast lateral movement well.

In 1971 I worked with an Argentine cruiserweight named Gregorio Peralta against Foreman in the Garden. I was working with Gil Clancy, an old friend, in the corner, and we were both shocked when Peralta boxed Foreman into exhaustion, then nearly knocked him out in the last round. If Peralta could do that to George, imagine what Ali could do with his slide-and-glide style.

Foreman was being trained by Dick Sadler, who was being counseled by the Ol' Mongoose, Archie Moore. However, when a man settles all issues with quick knockouts, he does not listen well to battle plans. Foreman was so confident that he had no contingency plan, no all-important "Yes, but what if . . ." plan. Archie, for his part, carried around a little black box that contained, as he put it, "the secrets of longevity, gathered from the aboriginal tribes of the outback in Australia." Yes, indeed.

Foreman also had a huge sparring partner who walked around

the ringside seats with a bullhorn incessantly repeating, "Oh yez, oh yez, Ali in three!"

Foreman tried a little psychology on Ali by making him wait ten minutes before he showed up. If he thought that waiting would work on Ali's nerves, he was sadly mistaken. Ali used the ten minutes to work the crowd. By the time the Mummy showed, the crowd was totally in Ali's corner. Ali owned Zaire on that hot night.

In the first round, Ali followed his master plan: lateral motion, feints, jabs, and some heavy punches to make Foreman think a bit. Foreman did not seem worried. He seemed confident that this annoyance would soon abate and that his siege guns would then reduce fortress Ali to rubble. Ali won the round, but didn't dent Foreman.

The following round was the shocker of all time for me. Ali calmly led Foreman to the ropes, spread his feet wide while leaning on the sagging ropes, held his hands up to protect the side of his head, and invited Foreman to punch. Like a thirsty horse led to the trough, Foreman began his work. Taking his time, measuring his shots, Foreman raked Ali's sides with deliberate, all-out, no-holds-barred punches. Angelo leaped to the ringside stairs; Bundini was pounding the ring apron. Walter Youngblood, the other cornerman, and normally a quiet person, was red in the face from yelling, and I was getting hoarse. We were all saying the same thing: "Get away from the ropes, Ali; get off the ropes!"

Ali's eyes were on George the entire time, and he was talking to him in a calm voice.

"Is that all you got, George?"

"That ain't much, Champ. You can do better than that."

"Man, that ain't nothing, George. They told me you could punch."

All the while Foreman kept up a steady barrage of long, powerful hooks to Ali's side. But amidst all the hysteria, you had a feeling you'd seen this before. Every day in the gym, for example. The Frazier fight.

The bell sounded to end the round and we all leaped in. Ali plopped down as a babble of voices hit him, all saying the same thing at different decibels.

"Stay off the ropes, Ali, he's going to kill you."

Ali waved us away with his quiet voice of command, saying, "I know what I'm doing."

I'm sure that in Foreman's corner, jubilation reigned supreme. After the fight Dick Sadler was quoted as saying, "Everything we planned to do—cutting the ring, overpowering Ali, going after him—was designed to put him on the ropes. And there he was. Exactly where we wanted him."

Foreman rushed to meet Ali for the third round like a man going to work after he's just hired Madonna as his secretary. Ali waited by the ropes, and in no time George was happily bombing away, but now, Ali was adding a wrinkle. In addition to the continuing dialogue, Ali began popping short straight punches, thrown with great force, his entire body behind them. George was stung, but shook the punches off, like a big grizzly bear flicking off some annoying bees. Suddenly it became apparent what Ali's plan was— and it *was* Ali's plan, born in his fertile mind as he measured his best chances in the heat of that humid night. Foreman would wear out if he kept throwing those heavy punches, Ali knew. In addition, as Ali had foreseen, Foreman, not the most mentally stable person at that stage of his life, was *listening* to Ali, and reacting to things Ali was saying. And he was getting dizzy from the head pounding he was receiving from Ali, whose combinations were brisk and on target.

By the end of the fourth round, Ali came back and reassured Angelo. "He's got nothin' left. Now he's mine. Now I can knock him out."

"Well, do it, do it *now*," implored Angelo.

"No, First I'm going to play with him a bit."

From round five to the finish in round eight, Ali had a good time. He led cheers with his free hand as he tied up a weary and dispirited Foreman. Ali had heard that his friend, Cleveland Brown fullback Jim Brown, now doing color commentary with David Frost, had placed a big bet against him. At every opportunity, Ali leaned over the ropes and chastised Brown for his lack of faith. Ali talked to the Foreman corner. At one point Ali took Foreman to his corner as Archie Moore came up the ring stairs to yell instructions to his fighter.

Ali looked at his old mentor, at Archie's bearded face, and said in a quiet voice: "Be quiet, old man; it's all over."

Foreman seemed to sag. Everything Ali did, psychologically or physically, seemed to have a devastating effect on him. By round eight, Ali was getting tired. The heat was intense, it was muggy, and it was almost 5:00 A.M. Clearly it was time to close the show.

With time running down in the eighth round, Ali started a five-punch combination—sharp, clear, precise punches. Foreman looked bewildered, shocked, stunned, and finally jackknifed onto the blue canvas and lay sprawled at the feet of Zack Clayton, who counted him out.

Foreman got up at the count of nine and then the bell rang. He should have been saved, but Clayton crossed his arms in the time-honored signal that the fight was over.

Listen to Moore, years later, on the fight: "It didn't make no difference: He was a beaten fighter. It saved him from a worse beating the next round."

I agree. Never was one fighter so thoroughly beaten as George Foreman was in Zaire. It afflicted him for years. He could not shake the vision of Ali on the ropes, of those sharp punches, of the blue canvas. . . .

Bula said Foreman asked him to come to his dressing room after the defeat and that there he confessed to Bula that he had seen Jesus Christ.

"How did he look?" Bula asked.

"Like in the Bible, with neon tubes sticking out of his head, all colors."

Bula left feeling that George Foreman had not acted right since he'd gotten to Zaire and that this fight had pushed him over the edge.

In our dressing room, it was V-E day and V-J day all rolled into one. As we started to our cars, the huge cloud that had hovered menacingly over the stadium burst and a monsoonlike rain drenched everyone. It flowed in torrents off the steep pitch of the field, and torrents of water ran into the dressing rooms and started to fill the ring. Ali's luck had worked overtime that night. If that cloudburst had hit minutes before, the fight would have been sus-

The quintessential Ali. *Photo courtesy Hy Simon*

pended. Ali would not have won the championship, ten years after he'd won his first.

The convoy moved through the rain-drenched jungle, happy and relieved. As we got into the deep jungle, we started to see natives coming out to the road, carrying their children and covering them with palm fronds or corrugated tin sheets. All they wanted to do was see Muhammad Ali pass by. Just see him. All the way to N'Zele the quiet natives lined the way, in order to someday tell their children that once, on a rain-swept morning, they had seen pass by: The Greatest!

Chapter 15

The Thrilla in Manila

After the thrilling victory in Zaire, Ali talked of retiring. For about thirty seconds, he considered it. Like a fading movie star milking an audience, he would throw out the thought, then lay back and await the sweet sound of his public yelling at him: "No! No! Champ, you're too young! You got years left ahead of you."

So Ali cranked up the Ali Circus wagons, now creaking from the overload of leeches, con men, relatives, politicians, show people, and the men of the media. Off the Circus went to campaign—Chuck Wepner in Cleveland (W 15), Ron Lyle in Las Vegas (KO 11), and Joe Bugner in Kuala Lumpur (W 15)—before finally the circle came round to its starting point: Joe Frazier.

By 1975, the boxing world viewed Frazier as a semi-shot, used fighter, although a name fighter who was still an attraction due to the reputation he had earned by beating Ali. Perhaps it was an unfair evaluation. Joe Frazier had lost in resounding fashion to George Foreman. He did look bad, but he'd come right back and beaten Joe Bugner before losing to Ali in 1974 in their rematch. Ali had handled him rather easily, but he'd bounced back again

Chuck Wepner decks Ali (briefly). Cleveland, March 1975. *Photo courtesy AP/ Wide World Photos*

Ali KOs Wepner in the fifteenth round. *Photo courtesy AP/Wide World Photos*

with KO wins over Jerry Quarry in New York and Jimmy Ellis in Melbourne.

At this point in his world travels, Ali had grown secure, confident that he could beat anyone, and he enjoyed the courtship of small countries that needed him to distract their unhappy populaces from political insurrection.

Enter Ferdinand and Imelda Marcos and the Philippines. Re-enter Bob Arum, King, Perenchio, et al., who held bits and pieces of contracts on an Ali-Frazier rematch.

And enter Cupid. Ali had brought back more than the championship belt from Africa; he had also brought back a beautiful companion named Veronica Porsche. Much domestic strife had ensued over Veronica's place in the Ali household, and the Philippines presented itself as a place to run off with her for some quality-time companionship.

In spite of Frazier's abiding hatred for Ali, Ali held Frazier in high esteem. Ali looked at him as if Frazier were part of the Act, as if he were the straight man in the big-time act of Ali and Frazier. The prevailing feeling was that Frazier was shot. After all, Foreman had obliterated him and Ali had beaten him easily in New York.

These factors contributed to the making of Ali-Frazier III, the Thrilla in Manila. But the biggest factor was that Marcos was willing to put up heavy money for the event, and the Ali Circus always needed big bucks to keep rolling.

The prefight madness included the finish of Ali's marriage to Belinda and the beginning of Ali's life with Veronica. Otherwise, it was the same hilarious show. Ali held court, minimized his training, and did the Act. Frazier hid from everyone and trained with the single-minded dedication of a kamikaze pilot.

The day before the fight, Vic Ziegel of the *New York Post* had these quotes that reflected the relaxed mood of the Ali camp.

Ali: "Joe Frazier is completely washed up. This is a pitiful fight. He ain't nothin' but a punchin' bag."

Bundini: "Third fight, third-round KO."

Ali: "Third round may be too damned long."

Angelo: "This isn't the same Joe Frazier. He's sluggish; his rhythm is off. Ali will KO him. I guarantee it."

I note with some back-patting modesty that Ziegel states that

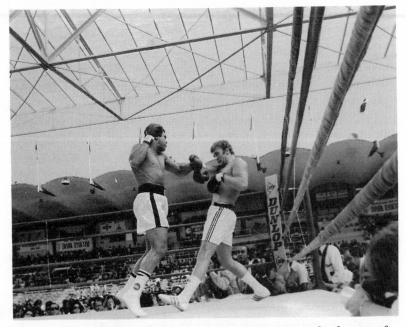

The Joe Bugner fight in Kuala Lumpur in July 1975. Ali won the decision after fifteen rounds. *Photo courtesy AP/Wide World Photos*

Joe Bugner covers up in the ninth round. *Photo courtesy AP/Wide World Photos*

the one voice of reason came from Ali's doctor, who was looking for a very hard fight.

Oh, yes. Yes, indeed.

Aside from the ubiquitous Muslim doctor (Dr. Charles Williams) skulking in the hallways with a tray of napoleons, cannolis, and other pastries, the prefight dressing room scene is quiet. It's nine in the morning, and the muggy heat is already unbearable. The Philippine Coliseum is not air-conditioned, and it will be packed, every space occupied. Outside, the hustle and bustle of the crowded Manila streets comes to a halt as the citizens gather around their TVs and radios. Manila comes to a standstill. The jeepneys and fancy bicycles pull over to the side. Even up in the hills, the guerrillas huddle around their shortwave radios. Ali-Frazier III, the Thrilla in Manila, is about to start.

Dressed in his usual all-white outfit, Ali enters, stares at Frazier, and circles the ring, around a large gold trophy that Marcos is going to present to the winner. As the announcer drones on, Ali steals the huge trophy and takes it to his corner. The Act is in high gear.

Joe Frazier is dressed in denim trunks, which look like a dirt farmer's overalls cut down to look like boxer's trunks. He looks right through Ali. He's seen and heard the Act, and he hates it. Hates being called ugly. Hates being compared to a gorilla (Ali went around Manila with a rubber gorilla in his pocket, which he would pull out at a moment's notice and chant, "I'm going to beat the Gorilla in the Thrilla in Manila"), hates being told he's shot, hates being told this fight is part of Ali's kindness, a "Good-bye Joe" charity event. Frazier had swallowed a lot of bitter bile. Frazier deserved, demanded respect.

As round one began, Frazier was about to get as much respect from the entire sports world as any one man could ever expect.

Ali, as predicted by many sports writers, came out flat-footed, his arms moving like pistons, bouncing his red gloves off of Frazier's head. Obstinately, Frazier stayed straight up, defying Ali to knock him out. Frazier buckled twice in the first round, but he did not go down. It looked as if Joe had had it. Ali punched with such force that Frazier's head was whipped from side to side, spraying those in the front rows with droplets of sweat. But Frazier was there at the bell for round two.

The second was more of the same. Ali meant to leave the Coliseum early; Frazier was ready to stay the course.

Lord, it was hot under the lights.

"Joe's still tough," mumbled a tiring Ali.

"He won't call you Clay no more," said the witch doctor Bundini over and over again. Angelo worked hard, almost in silence, as if he knew what hell lay ahead.

By round five, Ali took to lying on the ropes and resting on the corner turnbuckles as Frazier started to open up. As in the first fight, Frazier took inhuman liberties with Ali's ribs.

By the sixth, Ali was talking to Frazier.

"And they told me you were through. . . ." said Ali, pinned to the ropes.

"They lied, Champ, they lied," said Frazier, aiming a crushing hook to Ali's kidney.

The middle rounds belonged to Joe Frazier. Ali buckled under the merciless assault on his body. Evil left hooks caught Ali flush on the chin. At least once in each round Ali seemed on the verge of collapse. Ali held on to the back of Frazier's head and pulled him into a saving clinch. The referee, a small Filipino movie star named Carlos Padilla, had warned Ali against this illegal tactic, but he continued resorting to it. Ali needed a breather, Frazier did not.

So, at the end of ten, Ali had won the first five, and Frazier had won the next five. Ali slumped, exhausted by the heat, badly beaten by Frazier's body attack.

"I think this is what dying is like," he moaned. Bundini uttered a long, low groan as he passed the word to the worried Herbert.

"He says he's dying."

But during that sixty-second rest, the magic hands of masseur Luis Sarria were reviving tired muscles, and Angelo was energetically giving Ali a pep talk, and Youngblood and I were spraying him with cold water. Bundini, for his part, was praying some unintelligible incantation.

Across the ring Joe Frazier was listening to the sound advice of Eddie Futch, but Eddie knew his fighter was wearing out. Futch

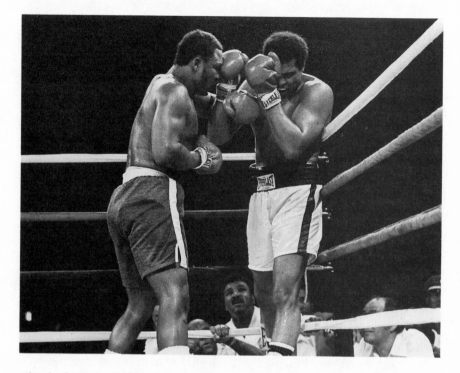

The third Ali-Frazier fight—the "Thrilla in Manila," when Frazier was TKOd after fourteen brutal rounds. *Photo courtesy UPI/Bettmann*

applied ice bags to Frazier's swollen eyes and nose. Futch knew his man couldn't take much more of the head-whipping he was receiving. It became a race of which would cave in first, Ali's body or Frazier's face.

The eleventh round was the high-water mark of the Frazier assault, like Pickett's charge at Gettysburg was the Confederacy's high-water mark. Frazier caught Ali in the corner, and spent all his last reserves in that assault. But when it was over, Ali still stood, and the world knew that this pretty face, this man-child, was one of the toughest men on earth—was, in short, a champion.

The twelfth round started as a continuation of the last, but Angelo's expert eye saw something. "My God, Joe's outta gas. He ain't got it no more," Angelo said to me, his voice cracking.

Ali seemed to sense it as well, and for the first time in many rounds he started to fight with his usual flourish and brio.

When Ali started his all-out offensive in rounds thirteen and fourteen, it seemed to me that he sensed destiny awaited. Ali's luck, which had apparently taken a break during those terrible middle rounds, was with him again. His long jab found Frazier's battered face. The right cross caught Frazier, and as his jaw flew open, a spray of bloody spittle hit the referee's shirt. Double left hooks rained on Frazier, who rocked back on his heels and then, catching himself, willed himself forward with coglike, rigid steps, willed himself toward this awful, punishing punching machine. Again the murderous combinations stopped him, and again Frazier reeled forward, hitting his gloves in front of himself, trying to get in close, to get back to Ali's body. The thirteenth and fourteenth rounds were the most epic I have ever witnessed, superseding battles of strength or athletic ability. They were more. They were battles of wills. They were fights for survival. There was only room for one on top, and Ali was there, and meant to stay there.

"Lawdy, that man can take a punch!" said Ali as he got ready for the final, and perhaps deciding, round. Then, we heard a roar from the crowd. It was over! Frazier could not answer the bell for the fifteen.

Benevolent, kindly, Eddie Futch had decided against further punishment. He knew Frazier couldn't see the punches. He knew Frazier was in danger of serious injury.

"Don't do this, Eddie," pleaded Frazier. "I want this, boss."

"Sit down, son; it's all over," said Eddie Futch, putting a gentle hand on the bruised shoulders of the warrior who wouldn't quit. "No one will ever forget what you did here today." And on that Lincolnesque note, the Thrilla in Manila was over.

It took a long, long time for the fighters to come to the press conference. Ali looked weary, bleary-eyed, exhausted.

"I'm tired of being the whole game. Let the other guy do the fighting. You might never see Ali in the ring again." Sound familiar?

The end in Manila saw a torn Joe Frazier shuffle off to a hospital, saying, "Man, I hit him with punches that'd bring down the walls of a city! Lawdy, Lawdy, he's great!"

And Ali, in his suite the next morning, said, "I always bring out the best in a man, but Joe Frazier, I'm going to tell you, brings the best out in me. Joe Frazier is one helluva man, and God bless him!"

Would that both men had retired after this fight. Neither would ever see this level of performance again. Frazier would fight one more meaningful fight (a fifth-round KO by George Foreman) and then hang up his gloves. He was lucky. Ali moved on like the Flying Dutchman of boxing, moving listlessly from fight to fight, his great skills eroding, his magnificent body falling apart, his brain absorbing needless punishment, until, in a ring in the Bahamas, the limb that Ali had been sawing finally broke.

Chapter 16

The Bloody Trail to Defeat, 1976–1978

Once the hematomas on his hips had resorbed, once the aches and pains had abated, Ali launched into a fresh campaign. The fights were dull affairs: Jean-Pierre Coopman in Puerto Rico (KO 5), a questionable decision over Jimmy Young in Landover, Maryland (W 15), a soft touch in Richard Dunn in Munich (KO 5), and then an experiment in the theater of the macabre—a title fight with a Japanese wrestler.

This bit of humiliation was conceived in the fertile brain of Bob Arum, the Ivy League lawyer who had abandoned law for boxing. Arum was a brilliant brain, but he has scant morals, and the chase of the dollar absolutely short-circuits in him any precaution or thoughts of harm, danger, embarrassment, or humiliation.

The Antonio Inoki fight in Japan was arranged in the spirit of fun. Few people took it seriously. It was done in the same spirit that Arum had hoodwinked the public into thinking that Evel Knievel was going to jump the Snake River Canyon in an "Our

143

Bowing to the crowd before a disastrous boxing-wrestling match with Antonio Inoki in Tokyo, June 1976. *Photo courtesy Luisita Pacheco*

Gang" rocket. Fat chance. Knievel bailed out, and Arum died laughing all the way to the bank. I've always felt that beneath every good lawyer there lurks the soul of a con man. Arum is a great argument for my case.

What was Herbert Muhammad thinking about when he accepted this embarrassment? Just money? Couldn't he see that the potential for humiliation was big? Had Ali come through the hells of Zaire and Manila only to become part of an absurd clown act? Even if Muhammad discarded the notion that it was not dangerous because it was rehearsed, didn't he see that he was endangering Ali's reputation? And, if it wasn't rehearsed, why chance his fighter's health with a wrestler? Especially one who could make his reputation by hurting Ali, by breaking Ali's bones, by spraining his joints.

Tokyo was one of those trips you'd just as soon forget. Just being there made me part of the swindle, and while everyone was laughing, I didn't see the joke. Neither did Angelo after the two camps held a rules meeting. Much to everyone's amazement, Mr. Inoki's manager recognized no previous agreement for a rehearsed fight. To him, it was a serious fight between a boxer and a wrestler—no holds barred. You can well imagine what that negotiation was like, as we kept forbidding different holds, kicks, falls, etc. Arum was defending Ali the loudest. "What a piece of work this guy is," I thought. Did he know that Inoki was serious about the fight? Had he sold Ali a bill of goods about a funny, rehearsed fight that Ali would win? This was no computer fight with staged scenes; this was for real. Had he told Inoki it was for real, and told Ali it was a hoax? We'll never know what Arum orchestrated. At the time, we only knew that Ali was in Big Trouble.

The "fight" was an abomination. Ali tried to fight with ten-ounce gloves, and Inoki took to dropping on the floor and kicking Ali's legs. Soon, the blood vessels in the back of Ali's legs started to break and pump blood into the leg. Two huge hematomas made Ali slow down. We iced them down as best we could, but next round Inoki was kicking Ali's legs again.

It was a long night in Tokyo, and one of the worst I ever spent in that beautiful city.

Ali won (won what—an exhibition?), but lost mobility in both legs. He had exhibitions scheduled in Korea and the Philippines. I told him to go home and check into a hospital. I informed him that clots could form which could go to his lungs, heart, or brain and kill him. As he lay in bed, his legs packed in ice, Ali nodded. Yes, he agreed, it was best to go home.

"Now that we agree, I'll make a prediction: As soon as I am out that door, the boys of the Ali Circus, the Hoovers [as the scavengers were called], will be in here telling you to go to Korea. I'll tell you something else: You'll go. Then I'll tell you the final thing: You'll end up in a hospital in the United States, and be damned lucky if you come out in a few weeks, and luckier if something much worse doesn't happen to you."

I'm no soothsayer, but I knew Ali and the Circus very well: All of my predictions came true. But Ali's luck held, and all he had to do was spend a few weeks in an L.A. hospital.

It was about this time that I first had twinges of conscience. I was not making money from Ali. I wasn't being paid. I had kept clear of financial obligation so I could do and say what I felt like about his health. The men around Ali felt he was indestructible. Everyone was caught up in a glory ride, and no one wanted it to stop. Ali was leading the charge, but signs of wear and tear were apparent. Ali looked worse with every fight. Judges were "giving" Ali close fights. There was no quality control, no control of any kind.

Ali was given only three months to recover before being

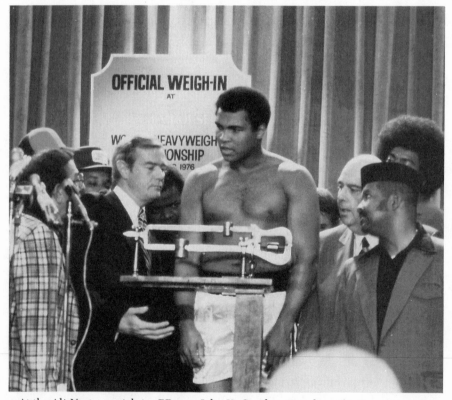

At the Ali-Norton weigh-in, PR man John X. Condon, Dundee, Ali, Commissioner Marvin Cohn, Herbert Muhammad. *Photo courtesy Luisita Pacheco*

matched with tough Ken Norton in Yankee Stadium in September 1976. Norton had a style that bothered Ali, and on the night of the fight he came prepared to take the title from him.

Ali was still suffering the effects of the leg injury, and his mobility was not what it had been.

The fight was in the open air of Yankee Stadium, and the night was cold and wet. Ali gamely fought off the determined Norton, but probably saved the fight only by his last-round effort. The vote was very close. Ali won, but the public booed. The feeling was that Ali's popularity and reputation had influenced the judges.

What did I think? Ali's luck, is what I think.

Back in the quiet of the dressing room, before the crowd poured in, I found myself alone with Ali. I was not sure he had won the fight. Neither was he, it turned out.

"I think it's time to call it quits. If I can't beat Norton . . ."

"Yeah, I wish you would, but you won't."

"This time I mean it. I've got to get out of this, before I start getting hurt," Ali groaned.

He would say the same thing after every tough fight; now, however, he was saying it with more conviction. Of course, it was not to be.

While Ali was thinking it over, he fought six easy exhibitions and one ridiculously easy fight (a fifteen-round decision over Alfredo Evangelista).

Herbert and the men controlling Ali assured me he would only have easy fights from now on, pick up major bucks, not risk his health, and coast to retirement. After all, there weren't any Listons, Fraziers, Nortons, or Foremans out there beating on the door. There weren't any lions to eat up Ali.

There was only one old lion: Earnie Shavers, and he was lying in the tall grass waiting for Ali to come by.

Chapter 17

Shavers: A Close Call and a Reluctant Exit

Time finally caught up with my conscience in New York City on September 29, 1977. Ali was no longer the healthy fighting machine that he'd been in his first decade of fighting.

In the ring, the sequelae of his tough fights with Liston, Frazier, Norton, and Foreman were evident. He was slower with each fight and took longer to recover afterward, and it was evident to even the most ardent fan that Ali was no longer Ali. Now he was a shadow that tried to look like Ali, but couldn't.

His training method of letting heavy-punching sparring partners like Ellis, Holmes, and Dokes pound his kidneys had accelerated the damage to them, and it was not uncommon to see blood in his urine. His speech had once been lightning fast; now he spoke slowly, in a seemingly more measured more thought-out fashion. The Act was now a tired repetition of old clichés. Even Bundini had lost his fire. The Ali Circus wagon was in desperate need of an overhaul.

I had had my troubles with Herbert and the Muslims, but it had just been the usual Ali Circus nuttiness.

At one point, Ali had insisted I accept payment, or a bonus, for work done. The boys in Chicago had told him that they were suspicious because I was living so well in Miami. Their ghetto logic was that I must be getting paid by somebody, and that somebody must be the other side. (Never mind that I had two medical clinics operating in Miami.) Nonetheless, Ali had insisted on paying me something.

At another point, Herbert did not want me to be up in the ring with Ali before a fight started. That proved to be the result of the Richard Dunn fight in Munich. There was an armed forces honor guard in the ring with the flag, and Ali was circling the ring, in his usual fashion, when the national anthem started. Ali stopped beside me. The NBC cameras were on him, with the flag off to one side and me in between. The nation saw Ali standing between a white man and the flag. The Muslims objected strongly, and Herbert requested that I not go into the ring anymore before a fight. I offered to go farther away than ringside—I offered to go back to Miami. Ali looked helpless, and when no one was looking, he said to forget about them and to just go in with him as I always did. But it's not easy to forget the Black Muslims.

The final insult came when Herbert sent over a bottle of milky medication one day with orders that I inject this substance into Ali, and not the fresh lidocaine-cortisone that I had just purchased that afternoon. The ghetto logic ran, characteristically, that since I wasn't getting paid, I could make a score by "doping" Ali and betting the other side. They'd seen too many bad movies about boxing.

Again I took the case to Ali, again he looked sheepish and help-less. I knew Ali well by then, and I knew how to handle it. I took Ali into the bathroom, ordered Youngblood to guard the door, and had a heart-to-heart with Ali, the gist of which was that I would not inject his hands with a medication I did not know and that if he wanted to go out and fight with unnumbed hands, that would be okay by me. Personally, my mind was slowly formulating a decision. The time had come to hop off the Ali Circus. I didn't like how things were going. It hurt me to see Ali going downhill so fast. It hurt me to see the insensitive manner in which he was being treated, and the ignorance of the obvious fact that Ali could not be put through tough tests like Earnie Shavers without endangering him and accelerating the neurological damage he'd already suffered. Ali was a gold mine playing out, a well running dry. The Muslims refused to see it; I did not.

Earnie Shavers was one of the hardest punchers Ali had ever faced. I'd seen Shavers flatten Jimmy Ellis, who had a good chin, with one good punch. To fight him now, when Ali was at his most vulnerable, seemed carelessly foolish, to say nothing of being aggressively stupid.

The first rounds were close, but Ali outboxed Shavers. It was not hard to move away from a man who was loading up every punch, who was gambling away points and energy knowing that one of these rounds he would catch Ali.

That round was the fourth. Shavers was all over Ali, who fell back, using the ropes to hold himself up. His eyes looked unseeingly into the crowd. Instinctively he held on to the back of Shavers's glistening head and pulled him into a clinch. Poor Shavers— he did not know he had Ali knocked out, and by the time he extricated himself from the clinches, Ali had sufficiently recovered to go into his escape act. The fourth had been a close thing, but Ali's luck had held out. Now he had to avoid Shavers until the cobwebs cleared.

NBC was televising the fight, and again the pundits of the New York press attributed to Angelo a gambit that never happened. NBC was giving the scorecards of the judges round by round. The New York writers maintained that Angelo had a runner going back and forth to our dressing room, where a TV was giving the score, and that hence Angelo knew the score as the fight progressed.

If that were so, then Angelo would have been the prize sap of all time (which he is not) for telling Ali we badly needed the last round. Angelo sent Ali out to do-or-die in the fifteenth, but the TV said that Ali was ahead on all cards and would win the fight if he just survived the fifteenth! And Ali damned near didn't.

Shavers, happy to see Ali willing to battle it out, caught him with some heavy punches. Ali wavered, held on, and came back fighting. His fighting spirit never faltered. Everything else was falling apart, but his heart was still that of a lion.

Ali won, no question about that, but he had hurt himself in other areas. The next day a New York Athletic Commission doctor, Frank Guardino, came to me and discussed Ali's lab work. His face was serious. The urine exam had not only revealed blood in the urine, but entire sections of cells from tubules. These cells filter the blood and make urine. They are not replaceable. They scar and impair kidney function. It is a serious finding, indicating impending kidney damage that could lead to grim consequences later in life. We sat together, comparing notes. He had been examining Ali for a decade. He had watched his fights. He had seen Ali's inexorable downhill course. How did he view Ali's condition?

He saw neurological deterioration, saw the same signs and symptoms of ring damage that I did. Now the laboratory findings had confirmed our worst fears.

"Ferdie," Dr. Guardino advised me, "you better advise him to quit. I won't make these findings public. If he comes back to fight in New York, I won't let him. You can show his management these findings."

I decided to try my very hardest to make Ali, Herbert, and the Muslims realize that it was time to quit. Ali had been magnificent, had done all that was expected of him and more. I decided to write a letter explaining all our findings, the lab report and opinion of Dr. Guardino, and my strong recommendation that Ali not fight again. I added one thought: If he ever fought again, I would not be with him.

I sent out five separate letters, certified mail, return receipt requested. They went out to Ali, Herbert, Angelo, Veronica (Ali's wife at the time), and Herbert's brother, Wallace Muhammad, who was now the head of the Muslims.

It was no surprise that I did not receive one call or letter from anyone. That I had expected. And when Ali wouldn't quit the exciting world of boxing, I did. If a national treasure like Ali could not be saved, at least I didn't have to be a part of his undoing. I hated to leave, and anticipated with dread the spin the Ali Circus would put on it and the interpretations that would be advanced by the press. Nonetheless, I felt much better after making up my mind.

As it turned out, I had not entirely abandoned Ali—I was hired by CBS to do the Ali-Spinks fight.

Chapter 18

The Spinks Affair: The Third Coming

Leon Spinks was a Marine who had won a gold medal in the 1976 Montreal Olympics as a light heavyweight. He had captured the heart of the nation by dressing in his dress-blue Marine uniform when not fighting. He was also funny in a goofy way: He had no front teeth, a wacky smile, a good-natured manner, and a fractured way with the English language.

CBS had hooked into Spinks, and had shown him in a series of dismally one-sided fights. When he got to his seventh, with Alfio Righetti (it was a draw, in a boring bout), talk started about a matchup with Ali.

I could not believe CBS was serious. As shot as Ali was, as slow as he was, he still had more than enough left to play with this windup toy.

Ali and his crew apparently felt the same way, for Ali barely trained. I saw him briefly in the Fifth Street Gym. He could not accept the fact that I would not be with him. Aside from the hand

153

The fighting marine of 1978: Leon Spinks. *Photo courtesy Luisita Pacheco*

injections, which were not indispensable, I had in recent years mostly been "along for the ride." The Ali Circus had grown unpleasant, and I would not miss the intrigues. Ali had that sly smile on his face as he whispered in my ear, "Yeah, but you're going to have your black bag with you, and if somethin' happens, you'll be there . . . ."

"I'll be there with a microphone, not a black bag."

"You'll be there . . . ." he said.

Perhaps I should have been. With Ali underestimating Leon Spinks, with scant training and a nonchalant attitude, he was cruising into the biggest shock of his career.

I remember the rehearsal for the opening of the fight show. We sat on a set in our tuxedos and talked about the three championship fights that would be presented on prime-time CBS.

Brent Musburger, the anchorman for the telecast, was his usual

Ali doing his Dracula number on Leon Spinks before the fight. *Photo courtesy Hy Simon*

glib, warm self, and I gave the opinion that Ali was in for a tough night and that Spinks could win.

Jack Whitaker, the voice of CBS's conscience, came on to say that the only battle that would be seen this night was a ratings battle between "Charlie's Angels" and Muhammad Ali.

I was amazed. I looked at him for a sign that he was kidding. Nope. Jack was dead serious. I warned him to tone it down some, since the possibility of a major upset existed. Bob Wussler, the president of CBS sports, smiled and shrugged, "Whitaker is paid to say what he thinks." I ran to Barry Frank, then VP of sports, and he also accepted the opening lines, which, it seemed to me, were downgrading a three-championship telecast that had cost CBS several million.

Now that I have been in the television business for twelve years,

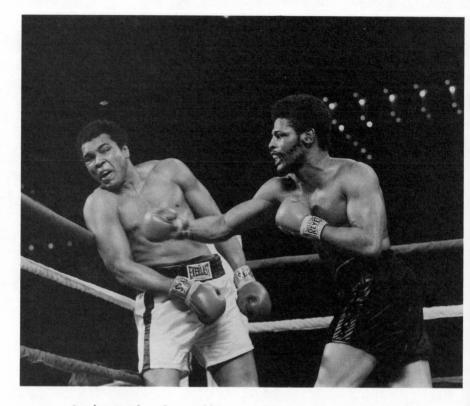

Spinks wins the title on a fifteen-round decision on February 14.

let me make some observations. It is an industry bereft of common sense. Nothing makes sense or has to. Its the only business where you can pay a million dollars for a product and then ridicule the product as fraudulent. Imagine Ford telling you its cars suck, or Budweiser ragging on its beer!

Spinks was an energetic, nuclear-powered punching machine who operated on hysteria. Ali was older, heavier, careless, over-confident, distracted, and, worst of all, uninterested.

The outcome was ordained. I had a rough time doing this fight. Brent Musburger was as helpful as any pro can be. He understood I felt helpless watching the ghost of Ali take this beating, lose his title to an amateur pretender. It was shameful, degrading, and sad. How did I get through it? I leaned on Musburger, tried to be impartial, and tried not to show my emotions as I saw the sad spectacle of what I was sure was the end of Ali's boxing career.

By the end of the fight, even Angelo had worked up enough nerve to suggest to Ali that the time had come to consider hanging them up.

However, Ali would never quit on a loss, so he made up his mind to train properly and to regain his crown. So it was that a rematch was signed for September 15, 1978, in the Crescent City, New Orleans.

The Second Spinks Fight

In the six months after Spinks won the title, he showed the world a side it had not suspected. He was a carouser in the Errol Flynn mold. Once he got his hands on the money, Spinks raced out to set a record in spending it all.

Imagine Bob Arum's headaches in trying to keep Leon Spinks out of the French Quarter and into serious training. The fun-loving Spinks would disappear for days at a time.

Ali trained diligently every day. I could see by his face that he was determined to show this amateur what real fighting was all about.

Again I was to do the telecast as an analyst, and Bob Halloran was to do the blow-by-blow. I think we set an endurance record that day for continuous talk. We sat down at five in the afternoon and didn't get up until eleven at night, having done extra fights on the card and talked through the intermissions. By the time Ali came in, I was praying for an early knockout.

The fight went as predicted. Ali played with Spinks, and Spinks fought a stupid fight. Leon Spinks had loaded down his corner with hangers-on and drinking buddies. The fights that broke out in his corner were better than the one in the ring. Poor Michael Spinks, his loving brother, walked away from the corner in disgust.

Ali won the title for an unprecedented third time.

I walked to the hotel with Halloran. We were both limp. Bob Halloran had been a TV sportscaster in Miami during the early days, so he too was a little saddened by the spectacle we'd just seen.

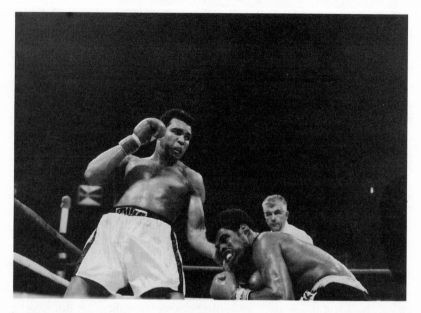

Ali regains the title for the third time. The Spinks bout in New Orleans where Ali won a fifteen-round decision in September 1978. *Photo courtesy AP/Wide World Photos*

"So, you want to bet Ali goes on?" he asked.

"No bet," I said before getting lost in depressing thoughts about the consequences of further fights.

"He'll never retire," I thought to myself. "Not now, not when he's the Heavyweight Champion of the Whole Wide World."

Chapter 19

Disaster in the Desert—The Larry Holmes Fight

Ali did indeed retire, in 1979, and as 1980 started, he was beginning to show signs of unrest. Ill at ease when he was not the star of the show, the main event, he wandered around the mansions of Beverly Hills in an ever-smaller circle. (Even Ali is subject to the laws of celebrityhood. The further one gets from active fighting, the fewer the invitations to appear.)

The Muhammad Ali of 1980 was still well known and respected. Ali may have retired as heavyweight champion, but he still felt he could come back at any time, against the top opponent, champion Larry Holmes, and win back the title a record fourth time.

Ali's uneasiness and dissatisfaction with being off center stage and stagnating in the Beverly Hills social scene was getting him itchy to return to the excitement of the Big Fight. Veronica, with her great beauty, her show business aspirations, and her growing social connections, had subtly pulled away from the time-and-energy-consuming grasp of Ali. Ali liked total control over his wives. When he tired of a wife, he found a more exciting substitute and manipulated his way into getting his wife to ask for a divorce. Sonji had been maneuvered into divorce by Ali. Ali, in the thrall of the Honorable Elijah Muhammad, had to make a deal to unload Sonji.

Belinda, the wife every Muslim dreamed of having, had also been maneuvered into an impossible position wherein she had to either get a divorce or live in an unacceptable situation. Belinda had been an exemplary wife—she stood by Ali when he'd had to suffer through the dog days of the exile years, bore his children, and exulted in his religion—and had given Ali no discernible reason to eject her from her position. But in matters of the heart, Ali has never needed a valid reason. He had found another in Africa, and had then manipulated himself into familiar territory. He created an incident designed to cause Belinda to move for divorce or else lose face. Belinda, the proud, wronged woman, came to Manila to find Veronica ensconced in Ali's suite, introduced as Ali's wife. Belinda fled from the Philippines to her lawyer's office.

By 1980, Ali was itching to change his life—and his wife—again. Veronica, now the wife of an ex-champion, was seeking a life of her own. Bright as she was beautiful, and in demand, Veronica could not sit around a mansion watching her hero rust away. There was no doubt about it: Ali is Ali when the spotlight turns on; but offstage, he is a quiet man, given to simple, quiet pleasures.

Ali enjoys eating large meals, then topping them with sweets of all types, mainly pastries and ice cream. This usually makes him drowsy, and when he's tired he likes to go to his study to watch tapes. His tastes in this area are also plebeian and simple. He likes cowboy and horror films. He seldom watches anything else. If he has company who want to see an old Ali fight, he might show it, but Ali basically does not amuse himself showing old fight films. He watches TV fights when he thinks of it, but he is not an avid fan of the game. Once you have been synonymous with the game of boxing, it's hard to see lesser fighters take your place.

When Ali traveled to the big fights to sit, hands folded, in his first-row ringside seat, he seemed detached and disinterested.

After all, no one could match his charisma, his excellence in the ring. When Ali watched the heavyweights, particularly Larry Holmes, he could not get himself to admit that Holmes, his old sparring partner, could be considered the Heavyweight Champion of the Whole Wide World. Not while Ali was breathing. Not while he still had enough for a comeback. Not while there were millions to be made. Not while the Ali Circus backed him to a man, believed in him, wanted him to come back and do it one more time. Just once. Just to show that Holmes was the King by the largesse of the Real King, Muhammad Ali. Not while activity would eradicate the ennui of the Ali household and propel Veronica back into the spotlight. Gone would be the boredom of the endless days in a mansion much too big for its inhabitants. In its place would be the excitement, the craziness of the Ali Circus in full swing. The all-night throbbing beat of a Big Fight in Las Vegas.

The Holmes-Ali fight was made, signed for October 2, 1980, in Las Vegas. Ali and the Circus were ecstatic. Once more Ali's luck would pull him through. Once more Ali would crawl out on the limb and energetically start sawing away.

Only this time Mother Nature, Father Time, and a Muslim doctor would conspire to make Ali lose before he even started up the ring stairs. He was knocked out in training camp.

By now the Ali Circus had grown to disproportionate size. Each man had his own clone, his own claque. They had grown fat and forgetful. They wanted—no, expected—their *windfall*. All they had to do, they figured, was perform ghastly parodies of their old duties. Then they would be rewarded by the spectacle of Ali winning once again, by big bucks, and by the comforting likelihood that Ali would enter into another mystical, magical tour before he retired again. The adding machines were working overtime as the Circus looked ahead to blue skies and green pastures.

First and foremost should have been the question of Ali's health. We have seen that in 1977 lab reports indicated that Ali's kidneys were disintegrating. His walk and talk were distinctly different, a sure sign of neurological damage. The Las Vegas Boxing Commission and other concerned citizens asked for, and got, a complete examination, to be performed at the Mayo Clinic. Herbert, as well as Ali, also wanted a full examination.

Now enters a factor that is not written about in the *New England Journal of Medicine*. What constitutes a full medical examination for an aging, disintegrating boxer? Certainly he is as unusual a patient as an astronaut or a fighter pilot. Regular, routine examinations do not show whether a boxer can box again. They do not *anticipate* or show his *susceptibility* to serious damage. When can a fighter be assured that each fight is not causing him irreparable brain damage? Brain tissue, when hurt, does not regenerate, it scars. Those scars cut through the neurons, which transmit the orders of the brain. Now you can *think* of walking with a spry walk, but you cannot do it. When you can think of words, you can't say them. You slow down. The condition worsens with age, it accelerates, causing you to walk like a sailor on a stormy night—legs spread, searching for the deck, shuffling forward. You speak in a rumble, your words indistinct and running together. Your face becomes flat, expressionless; your features thicken.

The Mayo Clinic, considered in medical circles to be one of the best, put Ali through its everyman examination and found him fit for combat.

One more factor comes into play, and it's a deadly one. No matter how casual medical personnel appear, they are human, and they respond to the presence of a superstar just like everyone else. They get flustered; they tend to favor and accommodate the rich and famous. Ali, who doesn't like hospitals and doctors, is at his most attractive, most amusing, most favorable when in a hospital. Doctors love him. No one wants to cause him any discomfort or do anything painful to him. Everybody *wants* him to be well. *Wants* to give him good news. It seems strange, but take it from one who observed this phenomenon for twenty years: Ali could charm a hangman out of executing him.

One of the interesting results of the lab test was that there was no evidence of hypoglycemia, low blood sugar, or hypothyroidism (low thyroid function). The diagnosis of hypoglycemia had been made in Zaire by Dr. Williams, who had also stated that he found hypothyroidism when he examined Ali in New Orleans for the second Leon Spinks fight. No laboratory evidence now corroborated these speculative diagnoses.

This becomes an important factor when one examines the almost criminal treatment Ali was subjected to in both fights. Ali was not then, nor is he now, a victim of either hypoglycemia or hypothyroidism. It is a grave error to give a man with a normal-functioning thyroid more thyroid hormone. The effect is to stop the pituitary gland from secreting Thyroid Stimulating Hormone (TSH). In other words, the pituitary is no longer needed because the patient is getting thyroid hormone from outside. The effect is that the pituitary shuts down its thyroid-controlling system and won't reopen. The net result is that a doctor can *make* a normal patient a thyroid-deficient patient—make a well man sick.

One last practical observation: The most effective judges of when a boxer is "shot" are the trainers in the gyms throughout the land. One good judge of boxers is worth a panel of neurologists. We Americans tend to lean on statistics and instruments. Would that there existed an instrument to test *athletes*. Unfortunately, no such machine exists, and none is likely to be invented. As an electrocardiogram cannot predict the likelihood of a cardiac accident, neither can an EEG, CAT scan, or MRI predict brain damage.

What should be obvious to even the most casual observer is that a complete physical examination for an aging boxer (or any athlete) is an inaccurate tool to gauge whether he can continue fighting without risking serious damage. That serious damage does not have to be acute (hemorrhaging, clots in the brain), but can be chronic (slow deterioration of the brain, leading to midbrain damage, known as the punch-drunk syndrome).

So Ali's disaster in the desert began to take shape. The pieces of the puzzle began to fit into their proper places.

First and foremost, Ali *wanted* to come back. No one forced him; no one even suggested it. Mainly Ali wanted to be Ali one more time. To bathe in the love and adulation of his public and friends while everyone listened to him in rapt attention. To "shock and amaze" the world once more.

Tagging along in the penumbra was the beauteous Veronica, once again in evidence, admired for her looks and position—and finally finding respite from the ennui of Beverly Hills.

Also on the scene was Herbert Muhammad, a man encumbered by a large family of offspring, a man whose finances needed as much replenishment as Ali's. A man whose spending habits were geared not only to satisfy familial obligations, but to add to the growing glory of the Nation of Islam. Herbert wanted to build a $5 million mosque to honor the memory of his father, the Honorable Elijah Muhammad, as well as to note his devout dedication to the Muslim faith. Can't argue with *that* motivation.

By this time the main men who had helped to build and then shared in the Ali legend were shadows of their formerly active, aggressive selves.

The main architect of this wondrous athlete was undoubtedly Angelo Dundee. He had planned him, subtly programmed him, matched him, babied him, supported him. But by the end of the run, he had become a whipping boy. The proof was provided by this fight. Angelo, the trainer of record, was not called in until one week before the fight. By then, the damage to Ali had been done. Could he have stopped it if he'd been there the whole time? Would he have interfered with the doctor? Couldn't the doctor see the sorry shape Ali was in? But we're getting ahead of the story.

Drew Bundini Brown had worn out by this time. Years of carousing, heavy alcohol and drug consumption, and his high, fast style of living had reduced him to playing "Bundini." Bundini was doomed to play out his life as a distant, diluted parody of himself. This fight represented a last life preserver thrown to a man swimming in the sea of his own bullshit. Poor Bundini, relegated to walk-on bits at press conferences, when he had been a prince of players in the company of a King. Alas, Bundini could not help Ali—or himself—now.

Luis Sarria and Wali Muhammad (Walter Youngblood), the quiet pair, had no role except to massage the King and to keep time at the workouts. Both needed the work. If they had doubts, neither would express them.

Of the other members of the Circus, one bears individual attention. The rest needed the work and the celebrity, since they followed and supported Ali blindly, which, all things considered, is as it should be.

The danger in this fight emerged in the form of Dr. Charles Williams, Herbert's personal physician from Chicago. We first met Dr. Williams in Zaire, when he maintained that Ali was suffering from hypoglycemia and suggested the "pie a la mode treatment" before the Foreman fight.

He reappeared in Manila with a tray of pastries, which were deflected to a hungry TV crew. It seemed funny at the time, but nothing could be done about it, for as I mentioned before, he was Herbert's doctor, he was a Muslim, and he was black.

The next time he emerged, I was no longer with Ali, no longer able to diplomatically deflect the well-meaning do-gooders who gave Ali diets, vitamins, vegetables, colonic irrigations, and a vast array of cures and "strengthening" drugs.

In New Orleans for the second Spinks fight, Dr. Williams came up with a new, and far more dangerous diagnosis: hypothyroidism, or low thyroid function. This was made with no provable lab test, although Dr. Williams did state that he took a "vial" of Ali's blood to New Orleans's Oschner Clinic, where he was informed of the low-thyroid finding. This visit cannot be documented.

In any case, this diagnosis is not made by running a blood sample through simple tests, but requires a clinical evaluation in which a radioactive iodine test is run. If hypothyroidsim is the diagnosis, it is one that usually sticks with the patient for life. It is not episodic. It doesn't go away, like a headache after an aspirin. Dr. Williams reported that after a short course, Ali returned to normal and thyroid therapy was discontinued. This is not consistent with the course of hypothyroidism. Usually, once you get it, you keep it. Period.

To give thyroid hormone to a healthy man is very destructive, as I have stated. In addition to leading to thyroid deficiency, it raises the basal metabolism rate, which then burns off fat and muscle tissue, and it raises the heartbeat. Reducing muscle mass in a boxer is like letting the air out of the tires of an Indy race car.

If there is one thing an aging fighter doesn't need, it's to lose muscle tissue. It is not valid to give thyroid hormone to someone in order to help him or her lose weight. Generally speaking, the fewer drugs you give a boxer, the better off he is. Old-time boxing trainers made the fighter run, work, and exercise off his fat, and they watched his diet like a hawk.

The older the fighter gets, the harder it is for him to lose weight, and the less power and desire he has to sacrifice. Every middle-aged person can relate to that. Ali, after the soft life of Beverly Hills, had ballooned to zeppelin proportions. Understandably vain about his appearance, and confusing weight loss with conditioning, Ali was susceptible to any "feel good, no pain" therapy. Thyroid hormone seemed a shortcut.

He also used diuretics to pass large amounts of water in an effort to speed the process. As with the thyroid hormone, there were side effects. In losing water, he also began to lose the minerals needed to survive a long, hard fight.

Ali's old spartan sense of self-denial had vanished, so to keep his appetite down he decided that amphetamines (or "speed") would help. In this instance Ali's vanity was greater than Ali's luck. He wanted to come in a little over 210, as he had in his first Liston days. As one ages, however, body weight fluctuates accordingly. His correct weight at twenty-one years of age might have been 210, but at thirty-seven years of age, he should, by natural progression, have weighed much more. No one told Ali this. In his "shock and amaze" mode, Ali thought of how good he was going to look at 210. No one told him he would be weak and ineffective at 210. No one told him it would be destructive to his general health or make him weaker, so that blows that would normally have bounced off his rock-hard body would now have maximum deleterious effect on him. If his kidneys were already falling apart in 1977, imagine them in 1980—then add to that the effects of Larry Holmes, a young, strong, huge heavyweight, banging them.

I began receiving calls from boxing colleagues, writers, and fellow TV reporters.

"Ali can't run four miles. He starts out, then collapses. Takes a limo back."

"Ali can't box four rounds. Has a hard time making three. . . ."

"Ali looks drawn."

"Ali looks wasted."

"Ali looks like a ghost of himself. He looks, talks, and acts weak."

The guys who ran the Ali Circus had phased out Angelo Dundee, but now brought him in to do his PR number. If Angelo had been there from the start, and had known of the thyroid hormone and other drug abuses, I am sure he would have had something to say about it. But by this time, who was listening?

Angelo Dundee had long since lost control. For years he was kept on because of Ali's love for him. Once a fighter gets to be a superstar, he tends to discard the "guy what made 'im." Then, he knows all that the man has to teach him. The star doesn't want to be reminded that he "owes" anyone for his success. "I done it myself" is heard in every gym in the country.

What Angelo contributed to the making of Ali was huge. It has been detailed at the beginning of this book. To Ali's great credit, he never denigrated that or failed to at least give a nod in Angelo's direction. But with the advent of the Muslims, when Angelo was demoted in favor of Herbert, Angelo's value began to shrink, and with it his place in the inner circle. As one of Ali's famous lines goes: "The wrong complexion, with the wrong connection."

Not that Angelo was "out"; he just wasn't "in" anymore. Now he didn't initiate orders, but *took* them. Meetings took place at which he was ordered to leave the room. A lesser man would have taken a walk, but Angelo is a man in love with talent. Boxing is his life. He had created the greatest fighter ever seen. Would he walk out now? Not as long as he was needed. But was he needed? Yes, oh yes. Boy, was he needed. There exists no better, no more complete cornerman in the world than Angelo Dundee. Ali needed his ring savvy, his corner generalship, his enthusiasm, his belief, his psychology, his expertise in cuts, his healthy effect on referees and ring physicians. We have seen specific instances where his "smarts" saved Ali: the Cooper fight, his blindness in the first Liston fight, the broken jaw with Norton—all would have been catastrophes without Angelo in the corner.

So as long as he fit in and was needed, Angelo would be there. Well, how about if Angelo saw Ali as shot and in danger of physical harm—would he tell him? No. Would he leave so as not to be part of the sad end of this once-great champion? No. What makes Angelo Angelo is dogged loyalty. "I started with him, I'll be there at the end." At least, fans reasoned, "If Angie is there he'll stop the fight. He won't let Ali get hurt."

But the Holmes fight proved the fallacy of all that, because along with his splendid loyalty, Angelo has another, dangerous side: He believes his own line. And that led to disastrous results.

So Ali entered at slightly over 210 pounds. The crowd gasped, the ladies swooned, the scribes scribbled furiously. "Looks like the old Ali," said one writer.

"That's the problem: He *is* the Old Ali," said another, more cynical scribe, understanding that weight has nothing to do with being a heavyweight fighter, and that old is old.

Larry Holmes was a young, undefeated heavyweight champion, and had earned the title by fighting a great fight with Ken Norton in which Holmes, fighting with a torn biceps muscle, outgutted Norton in the final round. He had fought all comers, and had beaten every one of them.

Despite all this, he fought in the shadow of Ali. Always he was compared to Ali, and always he came in on the bottom of the comparison. Holmes loved Ali. Ali had been kind, considerate, and generous to Larry Holmes when Holmes had been his sparring partner. Holmes, a decent family man, never forgot it. He hated the thought of fighting the "old" Ali, but such was the nature of the game. One day Holmes would be old, would want "one mo' dance, one mo' payday," and *he* would be the victim of a young champion (sure enough, a KO by young Mike Tyson ended his career—at least for a while). Now he was to play the part of the executioner in this passion play of the square circle.

In the week that Angelo had been in camp, he had not noticed Ali's apathy, his listlessness. No one had told him of the "pills" Ali was taking to reduce. Angelo was so busy doing his thing, which by now had been reduced to PR work, that he had not noticed Ali's flaccid skin and weakened condition, despite being "the trainer of record." Had he been blocked off so effectively that no one had *told* him of the drastic medication? Shouldn't he have seen it? Luis Sarria, the man who knew Ali's body better than anyone, clammed up.

So the aging Ali Circus wagons creaked into the bright lights of the casino ring. Holmes could barely look at Ali. Ali carried himself in a dignified manner. No high jinks now. He was an old man, full of dignity and posture, getting on stage for a final time.

"Ain't nuttin' to it but to do it," as Bundini used to say.

I watched the men gather around Ali. They looked like the old men you see at high school reunions. *We* were all old now, and only Ali looked young, but we knew, and he knew, that Ali was old, too.

There was an air of sadness around ringside that night. None but the most rabid believers thought Ali had a chance. Angelo had been spouting his "My guy is from another planet . . . he's not human" line for all the newsmen, and some, certifiable Ali freaks, believed it and wrote it. The English contingent, led by the capable Colin Hart, admitted their prejudice for Ali. Everyone hoped, everyone prayed, but almost no one *believed*.

The fight was beyond the nightmare envisioned by the realists. Ali had nothing. Holmes had pity. Holmes knew Ali would hate him if he took it easy and carried him, so he tried to make it look good, yet not knock him out. This would not turn into Joe Louis being knocked through the Garden ropes by Marciano; there'd be no knockout, if you please. But by not taking the quick, painless route, Holmes subjected Ali to a big, long, and embarrassing beating.

As the rounds wore on and it became evident that Holmes was carrying Ali, the fans and the press began to stare uncomfortably at the sad spectacle. "Stop the fight!" they screamed. "When are you going to stop it?" they yelled at the referee. Holmes refused to pummel the exhausted Ali as he leaned on the ropes for support. Time and again Holmes looked at the referee as if imploring him to stop it, but time and again the referee motioned Holmes to continue his destructive barrage.

From the corner, there was no sign of surrender. What was Angelo waiting for? There seemed to be a loud argument between Angelo and Bundini, but no sign of stopping it. Finally, by round eleven, it was apparent that only one man outside the ring had the power to stop it, and that man was Herbert Muhammad, who had hidden his eyes for most of the fight, unable to watch the humiliation of his best friend on earth, Muhammad Ali. But in the eleventh, Herbert Muhammad finally threw in the towel.

Why couldn't the referee have stopped it? Well, every time he started to, Ali would show some signs of fighting. Why hadn't Angelo? The extent of his delusion is contained in a quote from his book: "I don't regret the Larry Holmes fight, I regret the

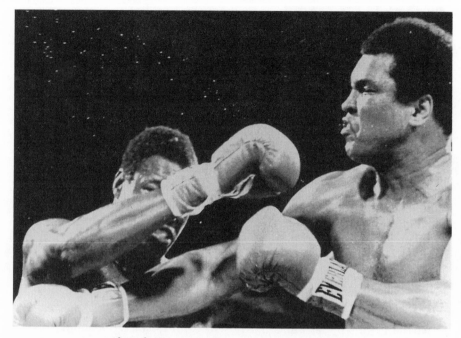

Ali-Holmes action. *Photo courtesy UPI/Bettmann*

Trevor Berbick fight in the Bahamas. *We could have beaten Holmes. We should have beaten Holmes.*" (Emphasis added.)

Now that, friends, is *loyalty*—the kind that can get you killed.

The Trauma in the Bahamas

As a sad postscript to the end of the Muhammad Ali saga, there came the incredibly shameful Trauma in the Bahamas, which Herbert should have stopped in its tracks.

It is a fitting commentary on this travesty to say that the highlight of Ali's last fight was not the shameful fight itself. The only newsworthy event of the night came when Don King got caught in a motel room and was given an island welcome by two "friends" of the promotion who carried brass knuckles and blackjacks. Don King lost one of the few disputes over his promotional rights.

Oh, and an average islander named Trevor Berbick decisioned an ancient Ali in ten pathetic rounds. So ended the Ali saga.

The winner and still champion: Larry Holmes. *Photo courtesy UPI/Bettmann*

BOOK THREE

The Ali Circus and Its Aftermath

Chapter 20

The Ali Circus

The Ali Circus was an amorphous mass of individuals thrown together at periodic intervals in claustrophobic togetherness, who strove mightily to achieve a common goal: the winning of a prizefight.

Between fights they would return to their homes and private lives to read the sports pages and wait for the first inkling that another fight was afoot, and then they would congregate again, ready to travel to foreign places or to stay in monastic isolation in the training camp at Deer Lake, Pennsylvania.

No book on Ali would be complete without a look at the members of the Ali Circus. It would take a separate book to describe them all, so I will devote this chapter to a thumbnail sketch of the first-string members, those who had seniority or were important in some way. As you have read, the making of the Ali Circus was a slow process of layering on and networking. It did not happen overnight.

Herbert Muhammad

The role of Herbert Muhammad in the career of Muhammad Ali is not well defined or understood. What is evident is the closeness of the two men.

The Honorable Elijah Muhammad wisely understood that Ali was easily swayed by any convincing con man, and in order to protect this valuable convert, Elijah decided to appoint his son Herbert as Ali's manager. What qualifications did Herbert have to manage a boxer? None. Was his personal record one of great success in business? Was he an entrepreneurial type? No. What had he done to provide financial security for his family? Herbert was a professional photographer. Was that enough to warrant his appointment as Ali's manager? No. His main qualification was that he was the son of the Honorable Elijah Muhammad. Elijah's advice:

"Stay close to this kid. The last man standing by Ali is the one who'll get him to do what he wants."

So true. So true.

Herbert was in a tough position. He had to replace Angelo Dundee, who had earned the right to "manage" Ali and who had a contract that would be hard to break. Ali's luck held here, for Angelo was not a man to worry about job titles or money matters. As long as Angelo was assured that he would work with Ali, as long as Ali was fighting, Angelo was happy. The financial significance of Angelo's cave-in is astounding when you consider the size of Ali's purses. But let's be practical: On Elijah's insistence, Ali demanded that Herbert be his manager, and that was that. Angelo really had no choice if he were to stay with Ali.

Herbert Muhammad is a quiet, almost shy man. Quick to smile, quick to laugh, Herbert is liked by anyone who deals with him. Grossly overweight and victim of a variety of serious diseases associated with obesity, Herbert lived through the grueling years of the Ali Circus world tour with the aid of pills and prayer. Considering his infirmities, Herbert did a magnificent job of keeping up with Ali and in protecting his charge from the many hustlers who were drawn to the Ali Circus.

Herbert had a strange relationship with his father, the Honor-

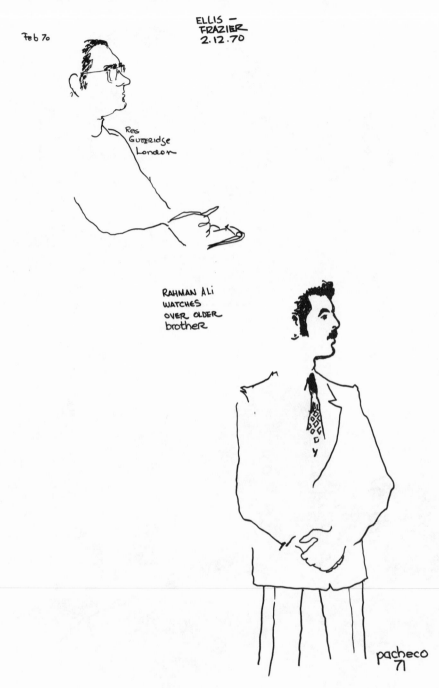

Feb 70

ELLIS —
FRAZIER
2.12.70

Reg
Gutteridge
London

RAHMAN ALi
WATCHES
OVER OLDER
brother

pacheco
71

The RAINS Came
miami Stadium
v NOV 76

Blood

Howard BINGHAM

Tom Gries DIRECTOR

Ali-Frazier NYC

SARRIA

Ali

THE HEALING HANDS—
paolino

DREW IN ARGUMENT
WITH Harry Markson
Frazier Fight MSG

Sonji

CASSIUS Sr.

DREW
BUNDINI
BROWN
1974

able Elijah, but the bottom line was that Herbert always succumbed to his father's wishes. Herbert protected his father's position with Ali, and in this he was helped a great deal by the reverential love Ali had for Elijah. Both Ali and Herbert got "spanked" by Elijah from time to time, but they never strayed far from his shadow.

What kind of relationship did I have with Herbert in those days? Courteous. Herbert and I always enjoyed a courteous relationship that was neither close nor distant. He let me do my work and did not interfere. Toward the end of my association with Ali, Herbert was being pulled in many directions by different men, and I felt that Herbert would be very happy if I disappeared—which, of course, I did. My present feeling for Herbert is one of cordial friendship. I know that he has come upon hard times in trying to complete his dream of building five mosques honoring his father. With Ali in retirement, Herbert cannot produce the heavy cash flow that the realization of this dream will require.

Did Herbert and the Muslims steal Ali's money? No; I don't think Ali was taken advantage of. Herbert earned his money. He made it the *hard* way. Herbert had to devote two decades of his life to being Ali's shadow. Yes, he was well paid, but it was *not* an easy way to make a buck. Ali always presented major problems, on a daily basis, and Herbert was always there to help solve them.

After the Honorable Elijah died, Herbert had an even tougher time handling Ali, and business matters in general. He surrounded himself with less-than-expert businessmen, sycophants, and a sprinkling of con men. Herbert survived this era fairly well, and learned enough to later help Ali out of the clutches of promoters like Don King and Bob Arum. Herbert dealt fairly well with both men, holding his own, and I think that neither Arum nor King had a complaint about how Herbert treated them.

Drew Bundini Brown

The main actor in this drama is without question Drew Bundini Brown, a Rabelaisian figure, a freedom fighter, a poet, a free spirit, a mystical force, a dissolute libertine, womanizer, and addict, a motivator, a public relation whiz, and a general all-around good guy.

Bundini was a tall, thin man, with a handsome, childlike, round dish face. His eyes could be intense and burn holes in the people he stared down, or they could crinkle in good spirits, or they could melt your heart when he was in his supplicant mode. He was a hard man to say no to, and hence fell naturally into the ways of a con artist and ladies' man.

A completely self-destructive hedonist, he could also not say no to Drew Bundini Brown. He conned and seduced himself into alcoholism, with occasional side ventures into drugs.

In Bundini's day, grass was a common staple, so he did not consider it anything but a mood-elevating, therapeutic agent. Cocaine and harder drugs were not unusual for Bundini when he was flush with money and had time to kill, but usually, during training periods, he was under control. If he did take dope, or get drunk, it was in his room, on his own time, away from the puritanical eyes of Ali and the Muslims.

Ali tolerated Bundini, and loved him as much as any mother ever loved a black-sheep son. He was Peck's Bad Boy and Huckleberry Finn all rolled into one. He was Ali's Falstaff, all bluster and jive, but he was also his soul mate. Ali could forgive Bundini any indiscretion; once, when Bundini stole Ali's championship belt and hocked it, the Muslims banished him for a few fights, but Ali let him back in.

While Bundini was aggressively black, and caused huge racial scenes in the South, he had a penchant for white women.

Among the many white women he "married," one bore him a son who went on to be a basketball star, college graduate, and navy jet pilot. White women were his thing, which was hard for Ali to justify to the Muslims, who had tough laws against miscegenation. In time, when things mellowed out, the Muslims worked out a way to deal with Bundini: They ignored him.

My first encounter with this aspect of Bundini's life occurred during the first Liston fight in Miami in 1964. One morning I opened my office to find Bundini standing outside my door with a pretty white girl. I recognized her as a girl who lived in the Mary Elizabeth Hotel and who liked to be abused and sexually assaulted.

She was from a good Northern family, and had run away to hide and seek humiliation in Overtown. Naturally, Bundini had discovered her.

"We'd like a blood test, Doc," he said, beaming his best cherubic smile.

"What for?" I said, thinking that perhaps one or both suspected a venereal disease. Everything considered, this was not a far-fetched thought.

"We want to get married."

While I had my nurse draw blood from the bride-to-be, I took Bundini into my office. It was 1964 and Miami *was* part of the South, with laws against integregration and miscegenation.

"Bundini, you can't get married in the state of Florida. . . ."

He drew himself up to his full six-foot-two, his eyes popping out of his skull, his mouth working to get the indignant words to start to flow.

"Doc, I was in the navy at thirteen, in the merchant marine at fifteen, I done traveled the world, seen me the pyramids, talked to holy men in India, done fought five years for this country, and they goin' to tell *me* I can't marry the woman I love!"

"Bundini, you are absolutely right. Come pick up the blood test tomorrow, go down to the courthouse, pick up your license, and go forth and multiply."

I was always very busy in my ghetto clinic, and did not have time to convince any Don Quixote that he was tilting with a windmill that would come back round and crack his head.

The next morning I arrived at my office to find Drew Bundini Brown seated outside.

Bundini was handsome in his blue suit, a flower in his buttonhole, but his eyes were tearing up, and his look was one of outrageous indignation. I took him straight into my office, expecting the worst. Bundini slumped in the chair and told his story.

"I take my bride and the two blood tests to the courthouse. I see this redneck cracker sheriff and says, 'Excuse me, sah, where is the license bureau?'

" 'Third floor,' he says, trying not to look at my bride.

"We go on up and gets in line. When we gets to the window I says: 'We wants a license.'

"And he say: 'Whatcha want, fishin' or huntin'?'

" 'No . . . I want a fuckin' license.' "

Bundini burst into tears of indignation. He began to sob, and his voice broke.

"And the cracker sheriff threw us both out of the courthouse!"

I tried to explain to Bundini the facts of life in the South at that time. After all, we had been fighting for some time to relieve these injustices, and with civil rights just around the corner, I explained to him, he was just a little premature.

It was not in Bundini's makeup to sulk over momentary setbacks. Within a day he was over it and back to living out the electric, high-flying days of the First Coming of Ali. The girl? She went back to her room at the Mary Elizabeth Hotel, the one with no lock on the door, and, having enjoyed a huge humiliation, returned to her life of small, but continuous, humiliations.

I cannot write about Bundini without enjoying the memory of his way with the English language. He was a street poet, a man who could interpolate the argot of the street into Shakespeare's English. Sometimes it was childish gibberish, sometimes it had a Zen quality, sometimes it was existentialist, sometimes a cross between "Amos 'n' Andy" and Damon Runyon. But, always, it was original, and a joy to hear.

During one of the rare times he was ostracized from the Ali camp, Bundini went to work for Floyd Patterson, who was training to fight Ali. The fight was set for Las Vegas, and I ran into Bundini at a press party.

"Doc, you always been straight with me," he said, gripping my hand in his two huge paws, his eyes popping out, his jaw set, his nose two inches from mine. Clearly, he was going to impart some meaningful information. "I know you are a bettin' man. I know, too, you are with Ali, but Doc, the chile got to be taught some manners. It hurt me to spank 'im, but he got to learn."

"You're saying I should bet on Patterson to beat Ali?"

"It's the chance of a lifetime. He be five-to-one by fight time; you can make a fortune."

I pulled my hand away gingerly and gave him a withering look of contempt.

"Thanks a lot for that jewel of a tip."

Bundini pulled back as if he had just received an arrow to his heart.

"Doc, I done put a C-note in the palm of your hand, and you done gave me back change for the Coke machine."

A last line from Bundini lingers in my mind. Ali had been placed in the Seagull Hotel in Miami Beach on a training trip. The Seagull, in season, is where the gambling fraternity stayed, and in the off-season it was a sort of nursing home for old orthodox Jews.

On this day Ali and I were waiting for our car with Bundini and two huge sparring partners. A tiny, matched-set Jewish couple came out and stood by Bundini for a moment. Now Bundini is a religious chameleon. One of his religious allegiances is to the Jewish faith, because one of his first wives was a white Jewish lady. Bundini looked down at the tiny couple with a benevolent smile.

"Going to the temple to pray?"

"Yes, it's the holidays," said the woman.

"Humph," grunted a gorillalike sparring partner, "tell them to pray us some money."

Bundini flashed him a hard look.

"Shit, man, if prayers was money, the niggers would own Fort Knox."

Bundini had talked his way into Cassius Clay's affection when the boxer was in New York for the Doug Jones fight. Clay loved to listen to the Big City hustlers; perhaps he felt a kinship, a brotherhood, with the fast-talking, colorful dudes of Harlem. Bundini, with his poetic rap, with his need to have a champion to attach himself to, found a winner in Cassius Clay. Bundini had been a part of the Sugar Ray Robinson entourage, and that captured Clay's attention, for Sugar Ray was his role model. Bundini told a story of Sugar Ray's needing strength before a big title fight, and Bundini's having told him of his closeness with an Indian guru who had taught him how to transfuse the strength of one man to another. He talked Sugar Ray into lying in bed with him, all night, in a chaste embrace, drawing all the strength from Bundini. In the morning Sugar Ray was brimming with the strength of two men, while Bundini was so wiped out he couldn't even attend the fight! Cassius Clay was sold! From now on he would have a fakir, a witch doctor, a man who knew and possessed secrets of the Far East, who could transmit secrets of the spirit. Bundini boarded the Ali Express.

Bundini died recently after being found in a Los Angeles hotel, in a $5-a-night room. He was a burned-out hulk. He was found paralyzed from the neck down by a stroke, and he died shortly thereafter.

Aside from Ali himself, Bundini was the motivator of the Ali Circus. And its clown. And its poet. And its fakir. And its witch doctor.

When Ali left boxing, Bundini left life. Perhaps that was as it should have been, for Bundini's life had ended up being Ali and his career.

Howard Bingham

If I had to pick a man to fill the bill of Ali's best friend, it would have to be Howard Bingham.

Howard Bingham was an unusual member of the Ali Circus, because Bingham had then and has now a flourishing and successful career away from Ali. His success has not depended upon Ali, and his talent is such that he can stand on his own and succeed. Bingham is a first-rate photographer, with extensive credits in Hollywood. He has worked for most major studios and was the favorite of many major stars, including Steve McQueen.

Bingham is a light-skinned man, with a kind and gentle face. He is affected with a terrible stammer, but, as with most entertaining people, one hardly notices it after a while.

At some point in his young life, Bingham decided to devote himself to being Ali's photographic Boswell.

This grew into such a slavish devotion that Bingham lost his family, electing instead to stay by Ali's side. Without fear of contradiction, I can state that Bingham possesses the most complete, detailed history of one celebrity ever compiled by a single photographer.

Bingham and Ali are like childhood friends who have grown up together, lived through fame, fortune, marriage, divorce, and children, and are now growing old together. Bingham is the only one who sits in continuous attendance. He is the only one of the Circus who fits the true definition of "friend," for he is a friend of Ali's and Ali is a friend of his. It is truly a two-way street.

Walter Youngblood, a.k.a. Wali Muhammad

This pleasant, light-skinned ex-golf pro layered in at mid-journey.

He came around and someone permitted him to keep time for the training rounds. He had a distinctive way of calling time, which came out: "Tooooooooooooooooooooime!"

He had an Indian look about him, was handsome, quiet, unobtrusive, and had a way with the ladies, the most visible being a gorgeous TV actress who played a detective's secretary.

Once, in camp in the Catskills, I sat between Bundini and Wali, and I was called to adjudicate a scientific matter.

"What color be blood?" Bundini asked.

"Red," I said, not having to rely too heavily on my medical expertise.

"No, man, what color be blood?" he asked again.

"Red, unless you are thinking about the blue blood of royalty — which is still red!"

Bundini was getting frustrated and flustered.

"Man, what color be blood?" he asked a third time.

And with this, he reached across me and picked up Youngblood's arm and pinched his skin.

"Oh, you mean what color be Blood?" I said, nodding sagely. Bundini nodded.

"Ochre," I said, not solving the problem at all, but extricating myself neatly from the argument.

Somewhere along the journey Youngblood converted and became Wali Muhammad, but he remained Blood to everyone. We alternated rounds in working the corner, since only three men can work in a corner at one time.

Blood was always courteous and smiling, and caused no trouble. He got along well with even the most contentious of the group. He regarded Ali reverentially and was intensely loyal to him — but then again, that was the one thing that everyone in the Circus had in common.

Blood and Bundini. *Photo courtesy Luisita Pacheco*

Luis Sarria

Sarria was an indispensable part of the Ali Circus. His function was to see to the fitness of Ali's body, and in that department he had no peer. Ali loved the quiet, dignified man, and Sarria was one of the few people in the world who could tell Ali what to do. Ali was no fool when it came to conditioning. He knew he had received a gift from God in his perfect body, and he wanted to keep it in top shape. He entrusted his body—and by extension, his health and his career—to the leathery hands of this guru of fitness, Luis Sarria.

Sarria was no unknown trainer working in obscurity when Angelo brought him around to help with Ali. Sarria had been a boxer in Cuba, and a famous trainer. He worked with Luis Manuel Rodriguez, Florentino Fernandez, Baby Luis, Robinson Garcia, and nearly all of Angelo's fighters. He was a busy man and the dean of masseurs.

Sarria was already an old man when he climbed on the Ali wagon, and the ride almost killed him. By the time he went to Zaire, he had a gigantic ulcer on his foot that would not heal. My memories of Sarria are of him sitting in our villa, foot propped up on pillows, the ulcer covered with evil-smelling unguents prescribed by a Chinese army doctor, intently watching a TV screen for most of the night. Considering that Zaire TV went off at 10:00 P.M. and for the rest of the night only showed a cloudy blue sky with a superimposed picture of Mobutu, I always wondered what Sarria was looking at.

He is now aged and infirm and living in a hospital, hooked up to a dialysis machine. Late in life, he married a lively Jamaican lady with a penchant for dogs. His house is overrun by thirty dogs. Poor Sarria probably feels lucky to be in the hospital.

If there ever was such a thing as a slave in the Ali Circus, Sarria fit the bill. In this case, however, the master loved the slave as much as the slave loved the master.

Luis
Sarria
2.12.70

Lloyd Wells

Every game needs a scout, a facilitator—a man who can get you people to serve you, to make things easy for you, to pleasure you when nights are long. Lloyd Wells is such a man.

Lloyd started out well enough as a college football star and then a competent pro football player. A talker from the day he was born, Lloyd, like Bundini, could charm the clothes off a nun. So it followed that when his playing days were over, he was hired as a recruiter. Hank Stram was the coach of the Kansas City Chiefs, and a man who knew talent, on the field and off. Recognizing that recruiting was a big part of getting a top pro team together (in those days), the coach hired Wells, who did such an outstanding job that Kansas City went to the Super Bowl. Wells wears his Super Bowl ring to this day.

When football recruiting became less important, leaving the resourceful Wells in the lurch, he found himself in a position to jump on the Ali wagon.

Using the same guile and tricks that he'd used to entice fullbacks and tackles to join the Chiefs, he found a place in the camp.

Like Bundini, Wells sticks in my mind because of his inventive use of the language.

In Malaysia, when Ali fought Bugner, we had nothing to do but carouse at night, then get to the coffee shop and compare notes in the morning. The coffee shop was like a campus club, and there were not many peccadillos that went unnoticed or uncommented upon.

At this time a politician from Illinois had layered on (and managed to get on camera at the end of the Bugner fight, which, he felt, helped him keep his political position). Lloyd, as was his wont, had brought to Malaysia his usual string of fine fillies. It would be hard to exaggerate their stunning beauty; in another era, they would have been show girls. The politician was drooling by the end of a week, and Lloyd suggested the possibility of a nice evening with one of the ladies. The politician eagerly acquiesced, and the evening was set up.

Needless to say, the morning after, the entire camp, all the writers, and Ali were downstairs to get the report. The politician came in beaming. Lloyd was the first to greet him—even panderers enjoy good news.

"How was it?"

"Most excellent."

"General Motors head, like I said?"

"General Motors indeed."

Then, within a few minutes, the lovely object of his affection came in and sat down demurely on the other side of Lloyd.

"Well?" said Wells, his mind on business.

"Well, what? He said this was a gift from you," she said, flashing the politician a nasty look. Lloyd rose to all of his six-foot fullback height and grabbed the senator by his lapels.

"Listen here," he said, his voice carrying all the way to the pool. "This here ain't no scholarship pussy. This here is pro pussy."

Well, the place erupted in gales of laughter, and now, anytime I see Lloyd Wells with one of his unusually stunning escorts, I think of "scholarship pussy."

Wells stayed on with Ali to the end and is now with Tommy Hearns. He lives in Houston, is well fixed, has some great antique cars, and is available for consultation if you have a fighter who needs to take "champion lessons." I'll tell you who needs Wells's street philosophy and down-home wisdom: Mike Tyson is a ship adrift and needs a captain to steer him through the seas of celebrityhood. Hire Wells, Mike. He's expensive, but he's good.

Gene Kilroy

Gene Kilroy came on the scene when Ali was at his lowest. During the exile, Ali was befriended and helped by Kilroy. At a time when few bad-weather friends were to be found, Kilroy was there.

Gene Kilroy is an unusually complicated man. He was a college football player, worked in pro football, was an army officer. He had the kind of Irish blarney that helped him to survive in any environment. He was big enough, and tough enough, to throw a punch when logic failed. A successful womanizer, he was and is a confirmed bachelor. He loved Ali from the start, sensed a great heroic figure fallen from grace in him, and came along at a time when Ali needed help. Not a wealthy man, Kilroy always seemed to have as much as he needed. What was better, he seemed eager to share whatever he had with the temporarily impoverished Ali. In this way, Kilroy legitimately belonged in the Ali Circus.

Gene Kilroy was the facilitator par excellence. Kilroy found Deer Lake and persuaded Ali to build a training camp there. It was to prove a magnificent move, as Ali trained for all of his tough fights up in those mountains, gathering his "family" around him and hunkering down.

Being a great instigator, Ali also watched fights between his followers develop there.

It was not easy being the only white man in a Black Muslim camp, but it must have been even harder for Kilroy, because he could sense an insult before it was said, could step on toes, could demean or savage a reputation with his sharp tongue. How he got through it all alive is a mystery, but he did have a few rousing brawls.

Today, Kilroy is the self-appointed Keeper of the Flame. He is very successful in a city that appreciates major league facilitators, Las Vegas. He is in constant touch with Ali. He invites him to fights, and zealously protects and guards him against real or imagined affronts.

Kilroy took an instant dislike to me, which has intensified as the years progressed and as my involvement in TV and writing developed. He particularly takes exception to anything I write about Ali, feeling it is a sellout. It is his tragedy that he does not understand that we all love Ali and that each of us, in his own way, is trying to preserve and prolong the fame of this unusual champion.

Still, when one writes about the Ali Circus, one has to recognize Kilroy's rightful place. When no one else was there for Ali, Kilroy was. And, even now, up in Ali's suite, you don't have to stare hard at the wall to see the scrawl: KILROY WAS HERE!

Lana Shabazz

If you have ever had a cook who was also an all-around expert in her field, who could dispense home remedies along with collard greens, down-home philosophy with ham hocks, who could love you, protect you, nurse you, and baby you, then you can appreciate what Lana Shabazz was to Ali.

A stout woman with a blinding smile, Lana rode the Ali Circus wagon in complete charge of nutrition and gustatory delights. The wagon did not move far without Lana, and every member of the Circus gave daily thanks for her bountiful gifts.

Like all the Circus members, Lana deeply loved Ali. She went to a fight and felt every punch. She suffered—oh, how she suffered—to see Ali hurt.

But that night after the fight she was available to fix this potion or that, this bit of nourishment, this portion of soup.

When the Ali Circus rolled to a stop, Lana regretfully walked away to a tranquil life as a school cook. She was not well, but she worked until her God called her. To the end she thought of her days with Ali, thought of the glory days when she was the Chief Cook and Bottle Washer for the Heavyweight Champion of the Whole Wide World.

C. B. Atkins

Atkins was a round man with busy eyes and a sonorous voice who used to advantage the business expertise he had garnered in guiding the careers of his two wives, Sarah Vaughan and Della Reese. He stretched a tenuous position into a living for fifteen years, largely through the generosity of Herbert, who seemed to need his advice.

Hassan

This small, round, Middle Eastern man was put in camp by Herbert to keep an eye on things. Mostly, he kept an eye on the dining table, and was never late to a meal.

Pat Patterson

Pat was a tough, big-city cop on loan from Mayor Daley of Chicago. He came to protect Ali for a fight and stayed on for fifteen years. Pat was one member of the Ali Circus worth his weight in gold.

If anyone ever had a better prepared, better armed, more experienced bodyguard, I would like to meet him. Al Capone was never
better protected. (Of course, the Chicago police force has had a
lot of experience protecting people.)

When the ride was over, Pat jumped off the wagon and into a
squad car to resume his life in the mean streets of the Windy City,
the roar of the Big Event crowds still ringing in his head above
the sounds of the police siren.

James Anderson

James was an extension of Pat without the professional training.
He was quiet, but firm. He kept order. He was trustworthy. He
is now with the Tommy Hearns camp serving in a similar bodyguard capacity.

There were many characters who came and went (and some who
disappeared), who lingered in favor for a fight or two, then lost
their grip and fell off.

The Louisville Group with Bill Faversham lasted until the Liston fight; Bill MacDonald bankrolled many a Chris Dundee fight,
but he too dropped by the wayside after the Liston brawl. With
Angelo at all the fights was his dapper brother Jimmy. He was a
fashion plate, and he had an even softer heart than Angelo. He
kept Angelo from giving away all the money, and all the tickets.
Some pair. They were both soft touches. Jimmy stayed on until he
died of cancer at an early age. He was loved by all, and missed
when he was gone.

Harold Conrad, the fast-talking ex-sportswriter, promoter, and
PR man, was with us at the start. The Humphrey Bogart part in
Schulberg's *The Harder They Fall* was based on the character of
Harold Conrad. He was with Ali in the early days, but the Muslims
were not big Damon Runyon fans, so Gentleman Harold went his
way when the time came.

The Muslims sent over a few characters who lingered and remained in camp. Names like Booker Griffin, Abdul Rahaman
(Cap'n Sam), Faird D. Salaam, Booker "Abubakiur" Johnson, who
always carried a Bible—or was it the Koran?

I loved the hustlers. They were many. Few succeeded in major larcency. Some tried, but they ceased to exist.

One slim, dapper con who layered in during the Jerry Quarry fight in Atlanta was Major (or Colonel, depending on who he was talking to) Coxson. He got close to Ali, and I could hear cash registers chiming in his ears.

"What are you going to sell him, Major, a house?" I asked him during one nocturnal walk.

"Nah. Bigger'n that. I got me a whole block of downtown Detroit we can pick up for back taxes. Chicken feed."

"Watch out if your arithmetic is not straight, Major. These guys around Ali haven't got a good sense of humor."

Major Coxson hung around for a few fights, eventually sold Ali a block of downtown somewhere that turned out to be encumbered with mortgages and huge taxes—and condemned in the bargain. Major Coxson got involved in some internecine theological disagreement. Someone killed Major Coxson, his wife, and five children.

Reggie was a short, wiry, nervous driver-secretary who was funny in those early Liston days. The Muslims didn't find him too funny, and he disappeared after a disagreement over mathematics. Some say he is part of the ecology enrichment of the Okefenokee swamp. I wouldn't know. I just haven't seen him since the disagreement.

Live Wire was a flashy, heavy dude from Detroit who had a gold tooth with a diamond in its center.

One of the ways that Live Wire made a living was customizing cars and limos. He hung around for a few fights, then got Herbert in his sights and offered him a great deal on a customized limo. When he was finished, he delivered it to Herbert in Chicago. The trouble was, the Drug Enforcement Administration boys were waiting. They tore down the limo and found large packages of white powder, which on laboratory analysis proved not to be detergent powder. Live Wire was sent to a penitentiary to do hard time. Herbert, the most drug-free, alcohol-free person I know, was chagrined. Herbert and the Muslims could have been embarrassed and publicly condemned. Feelings were hard. Live Wire did not make it out of jail. He died in "a mathematics argument" in the yard one day.

The Geechie, Reggie Thomas, layered on. What he did no one knew. He was a light-skinned, straight-haired, green-eyed man, and very likable. He used Ali to stage some exhibitions and, later, he was caught with an inordinate amount of white powder in his car. Ali, in his fashion, stood up for the Geechie at his trial. But the DEA did not listen to Ali, and the Geechie left the Circus to stamp out license plates for the state of South Carolina.

Harold Ross Smith (real name, Ross Fields) has to be considered the premier con artist to ever matriculate through the Ali Circus. We all knew he was hanging bad paper all over Texas, but the Ali Circus was moving too fast to worry about types like Harold.

After Ali retired, Harold sold NBC a series of fights between Ali's amateur fighters and Frazier's fighters. It was a sound concept, backed by Ali's name. The problem was that Harold had no funds, and NBC didn't pay until after an event.

Now Harold Ross Smith was a creative mathematical genius, and he had one more advantage: He had considerable influence over a vice president inside the Wells Fargo Bank.

Harold Ross Smith had found an inexhaustible supply of the "ready." From that point, he launched on a sleigh ride that stunned the imagination of even the wildest member of the Ali Circus. He ended up doing time in a federal penitentiary over a disagreement with the government concerning a financial problem. Ali stood by him, enjoying the machinations of this unusual con man.

The best line I ever heard from Harold came when he was about to go on trial.

"They'll never convict me, Doc. If a street nigger like me can get into a bank and manipulate the computers, and take out twenty-three million dollars, imagine what those white motherfuckers in their three-button suits are doing with those computers!"

Harold Ross Smith was right. He was the tip of the iceberg we are now seeing with the savings and loans scandals, and the junk-bond manipulations, and the rest of the uses of creative bookkeeping.

But we were not assaulted only by street hustlers. We had a

dentist in Houston who wanted to join the Circus and make mouth-pieces for Ali. We had a tiny, megalomaniacal neurosurgeon from Washington, D.C., who wanted to sign on. Lawyers came in waves. Writers, photographers, painters all flocked to Ali's side. Only Leroy Neiman had the guts, talent, and stick-to-itiveness to become Ali's painter. It fills me with sadness to know that some unthinking clod has painted over the walls of the Deer Lake gym, which contained priceless Neiman sketches of Ali, including a life-size drawing in white paint. Progress. Damn them.

For a brief moment, Herbert hired Richard Durham to do a biography, which took longer to write than it took to finish World War II.

Immediately he was tagged "Hemingway," and his abrasive way did not endear him to the Circus. To begin with, he maintained that he was not a Muslim. Considering that he was an editor of *Muhammad Speaks*, the official Muslim newspaper, this seemed as ridiculous as maintaining that the pope is not Catholic. Hemingway hung around, stirring up phony scenarios with racial themes, trying to write pathetic revisionist history, making Ali a cross between Martin Luther King, Dred Scott, and Joan of Arc. The book he finally delivered had to be heavily edited by its publisher and does not present the Muhammad Ali I know. Hemingway must have read his critics, because shortly thereafter he married a wealthy woman, and so far is living happily ever after.

White liberal kids would layer on as teenagers and stay on into their adulthood. One kid, who appeared pretty regular when he started in Miami, had a full head of hair, a full beard, and a Western fringed jacket when I next met him. Immediately he became "Buffalo Bill." Today, he is prosperous as a manager of two Germans who seem to have a way with tigers. His real name is Bernie Youmans, but ask any Ali Circus rider and instantly you'll be told his real name is Buffalo Bill.

One character I particularly loved was a very tall man who was simply named Flip. Flip was the real-life model for Woody Allen's film *Zelig*. Wherever there was a winner's circle—be it a Kentucky Derby finish line, a World Series locker room, a Super Bowl dressing room, or around Ali as he stood, arms uplifted, in triumph—there was the tall, dapper Flip.

"In 1941 I was living at home in St. Louis. I came home and found a letter from the U.S. Army. Drafted. Well, I put it on the mantel, and as far as I know, it's still there." Flip would laugh as he told the story.

Flip never asked for anything. He was just there, at every fight. Whether it was Africa, Malaysia, Jakarta, Europe, Asia, or Cleveland, there was Flip.

Last year, headed for the auditorium to see a Tyson championship fight, I heard that Flip had died of a heart attack on his way to the fight. Saddened, I started to walk to my seat, and found myself face-to-face with Ali.

Ali's reaction was slow as he put his big hand on my shoulder, a smile slowly spreading on his handsome face.

"Doc, we're all getting old. Things are catching up with us."

We laughed together a moment, then began telling Flip stories, enjoying the memory of this unusual man. Finally, Ali shuffled off, walking slowly, hands shaking, nodding, and I stopped laughing.

On that somber note, and with apologies to all of those who rode with the Ali Circus but whose faces and names are buried by time, I close this chapter. In retrospect, I can only say this about the Ali Circus: I loved every crazy moment of it.

Chapter 21

The Punch-drunk Syndrome: Questions and Answers

What is a shot fighter?

Sugar Ray Robinson, who boxed far beyond his time, described it best in one sentence: "I can see a jab coming and I can't block it, and I can see an opening to land a jab but by the time my brain sees it and recognizes it, the opportunity is gone."

There it is in a nutshell. The boxer's reflexes are no longer what they were. This applies as well to the legs—they no longer carry him out of range, or support him through a tough fight.

Since the brain has also aged, and been hurt, the boxer's ability to take a punch is diminished. One of the champions I worked most closely with was Luis Manuel Rodriguez, and he had a rock for a chin. After he had had over eighty fights, and was in his thirties, Luis fought a rematch with an ordinary Mexican fighter whom Luis had knocked out six months earlier. Suddenly Luis was being hit by every jab this boxer threw, and by the end of round one, he had already been knocked down. Luis wound up being TKO'd in an early round. Overnight, Luis Manuel Rodriguez was shot. He tried three more fights and retired. He was lucky.

What medical examinations can be conducted to prove that a fighter is shot?

Unless the deterioration is in its final, evident stages, there is no examination to show that an athlete has lost his skills. Unlike the way it is in other sports, in boxing this is disastrous, because it is during the last bouts of a fighter's career that the damage leading to the punch-drunk syndrome occurs.

What about CAT scans, electroencephalograms (EEGs), and magnetic resonance imaging (MRI)?

These are used to reveal an injury, not to predict it or to measure a loss of athletic ability. I've never heard of a machine that can measure a man's capacity to take a punch. No one can measure the brain's ability to absorb a shock. In boxing one has to factor in heart, guts, the will to win, and the will to not go down. Jake LaMotta's brain is anatomically the same as Floyd Patterson's, yet Jake had a perverse pride in not going down, no matter how rough the beating, as he showed in the sixth Robinson fight, whereas Patterson was down in almost every one of his fights.

Why?

No machine will give the answer.

Who is the best judge of when a fighter is "shot"?

Gym rats—trainers, managers, and fight people who go to a gym on a daily basis and observe fighters in training.

Doctors who see a fighter once, on the day of the fight, cannot begin to compare with them as judges of the deterioration of a fighter.

A fighter who is in excellent health, by routine physical examination, can still be a "shot" fighter in the ring.

Who is the worst judge of when a fighter is shot?

Promoters and managers, whose judgment is confused by profit-and-loss statements. The more valuable a fighter is, the blinder the promoter and manager get. Check the careers of Muhammad Ali, Joe Louis, Sugar Ray Robinson, Archie Moore, Sugar Ray Leonard, etc.

Should shot fighters be allowed to fight a few "easy" fights to ease them out of boxing gradually?

When a boxer is shot, his susceptibility to brain damage is greater by far than when he was young. It sounds humane to allow a famous fighter to fight a few easy fights, pick up big bucks, and get out. It *never* works that way.

Witness the "easy" fights that were given Ali: Earnie Shavers(!), followed by Leon Spinks, then Larry Holmes. Easy fights? There are none.

Easy fights sound deceptive. The killer is, you still have to train, and this entails daily sparring, which entails getting hit in the head. Easy fights?

What exactly is the punch-drunk syndrome?

When a fighter has sustained midbrain damage, the symptoms are:

Loss of proprioception: A big word that means "balance," based on the signals the brain gets that tell you where you are in relation to the earth. It's so basic no one is aware of it. It tells you if you are standing straight or leaning, if you are lying down, sitting, standing up.

In the PDS (punch-drunk syndrome), this has been disturbed. There is an instinctive need to "find" the earth. You walk like a sailor on a ship in the middle of a storm. Feet spread apart, shuffling, and a slower walking-gait are what one sees in PDS. Go down to your local gym and watch old fighters (with long records) walk around.

Flattened face: The face is essentially expressionless, because the nerves that run to the muscles of expression no longer trigger off signals to make them move. Punch-drunk fighters generally have flat faces.

Thickened voice: The voice is now a rumble, or gravelly, raspy.

Loss of ability for verbal expression: The fighter is slow in thinking of words. In the case of advanced midbrain damage, the brain can find the word but can't get it out to say it.

Slowness of speech: There is an inability to form rapid thoughts and to enunciate the thoughts that finally do get through.

Slowness in understanding: The fighter will have difficulty comprehending what is being said to him.

Loss of blink reflex: An inability to blink means that the eyes get dry, tired, and heavy. This, in concert with the decreased brain function, results in a man who falls asleep frequently and in public.

Psychiatric problems: The onset can be gradual and occur over a number of years. There is frequent cheerful or fatuous affect associated with the dementia, though violent behavior and paranoia are present in some.

Decrease of memory: The ability to recall is impaired, with diminished insight into problems.

Tremors: These are due to the same motor (muscle) disorder that affects motion and movement.

Dr. M. Critchley, in the *British Journal of Medicine* in 1957, listed these signs and symptoms in his dissertation, "The Medical Aspects of Boxing," and gave a differential diagnosis: Parkinson's disease, frontal-lobe tumor, and multiple sclerosis.

Since 1928, when the punch-drunk syndrome was first observed and studied, many reports have followed. Periodically a highly visible old champion suffers a highly visible decline, and then the studies speed up once again.

Within the span of a few years, Joe Louis developed advancing mental decline and Sugar Ray Robinson became a victim of Alzheimer's disease and died. Muhammad Ali progressed with shocking rapidity from boxing-induced neurological damage to a Parkinson-like symptomatology.

Boxing apologists immediately claimed that Joe Louis's problems stemmed from drugs, Robinson's from old age, and Ali's from Parkinson's disease.

It is both bewildering and discouraging that supposedly intelligent men, without benefit of a medical education or practical clinical experience—or even, in the case of two boxing analysts, any behind-the-scenes boxing background—can airily dismiss boxing as the prime cause of these disorders.

In a recent article by Dr. Joseph H. Friedman in the *Southern Journal of Medicine*, there is a review of the literature which deduces that the damage caused by boxing (read "staying on too long") can (and does) progress to Parkinson's disease. Also, Friedman says, "There are at least two points of theoretic interest in this syndrome relevant to our understanding of other degenerative brain disorders. These are the presence of *neurofibrillary tangles* in the cortex of former boxers, and the delayed onset of signs and symptoms." The questions of how repeated head blows cause neurofibrillary tangles, and how they compare with the same neurofibrillary tangles found in Alzheimer's, are being carefully studied.

Dr. Friedman again: "In boxing one can hypothesize either that boxing injuries have caused a loss of redundancy in the brain or that the boxing injuries have set in motion a series of events that produce a degenerative brain disease."

Studies are now accelerating due to the use of EEGs, CAT scans, and (in my opinion, the best) magnetic resonance imaging (MRI). It is safe to assume that the theories set forth by Dr. H. S. Martland based on the first study of long-range effects of boxing on the brain, in the *Journal of the American Medical Association* (JAMA) in 1928 are now being proven conclusively. With boxers living longer, we are seeing the end results, which appear to be a progression into Parkinson's disease or, in worse cases, Alzheimer's.

The reader who has plowed through the medical facts must, perforce, think of the sad case of Muhammad Ali since, unfortunately, he is the most highly visible victim of his sport, and suffers in the most public way.

At the start, let me say that I lead the way in feeling badly for the former champion. Not sorry. I do not have pity. To do so would be to hurt Ali, for he is a proud man, a man of great equanimity, and a man whose last wish would be for anyone to feel either pity or sorrow for him.

Ali picked his road. He was told clearly of the risks he was taking, and so were his managers and handlers. They chose to ignore the possibilities of serious damage and rode the Ali Circus to the end. This was a unanimous choice.

None of them jumped off the Ali wagon. Although I don't agree with their decision, I understand it. Life must go on. Chances must be taken. A man has a right to do what he thinks is right. And, sometimes, greed is greed.

Learning to paint after his retirement. The picture is signed. *Photo courtesy Hy Simon*

This I understand and do not object to. What I *do* strenuously object to is that now, when living evidence of the Circus members' and other supporters' mistake is before them, in the figure of an injured and ill Ali, they are all screaming in unison:

"He has Parkinson's disease; boxing had nothing to do with it."

I can understand the rationalization of the Ali Circus; after all, most of them must have some twinges of conscience. But I do not understand TV analysts like Alex Wallau, who claimed in an interview in *KO* magazine that Ali was not injured in boxing, but that, coincidentally, unrelated to boxing, he has Parkinson's disease. A similar position has been maintained by Larry Merchant of HBO.

Curiously, these two men are equal in the absence of credentials that would give them the right, or the knowledge, to make such injurious disclaimers. Neither man has medical training, clinical background, or boxing experience other than as periodic observers of the scene.

By taking these frivolous attitudes on national TV, they undermine the work of boxing commissions and medical researchers who are struggling to limit the damages caused by a fighter's boxing past his prime. Boxing should be curtailed. The less you box, the less the possibility of the PDS, Parkinson's disease, and maybe even Alzheimer's disease.

Chapter 22

Ali's Place in History

Any student of fistic history has to place Ali's name at the top of the list of boxers who transcended the sport, who improved and deeply influenced it.

Muhammad Ali was clearly made for the electronic age. He emerged as new technology was developing that gave him the possibility, hitherto unthought of, of appearing on a worldwide stage. He possessed all the attributes of a perfect hero: He was young, handsome, brash, witty, irreverent, chance-taking, religious, clean, and entertaining. But, best of all, he was simply, far and away, the greatest fighter of his time.

Ali's adoption of the Muslim faith brought him millions of new fans who would never have heard of him otherwise. It banded him closer to his black brothers and sisters in America. The white liberals adored him.

Then Ali took a step many considered a big mistake: He refused to be inducted into the U.S. Army. His simple "I ain't got no quarrel with them Vietcong" became a rallying cry for the young of America. He was exiled, and the Honorable Elijah Muhammad even threw him out of the religion, forbidding him the use of his

Muslim name. But Ali persisted in using his Muslim name, and overcame Elijah's and America's punishments, and achieved a new height of popularity.

Then came the Second Coming of Ali and the epic battles, each a classic to be cherished and appreciated for as long as fans look at boxing. The first Ali-Frazier ("The Fight"); Ali-Norton (the broken jaw); Ali-Foreman ("Rumble in the Jungle"); the third Ali-Frazier ("Thrilla in Manila"); the third Ali-Norton in Yankee Stadium; and the second Ali-Spinks, where Ali won back the heavyweight title for the third time.

And the years flew by and generations grew up recognizing only one name as being synonymous with "Champion," and that was Muhammad Ali.

Ali was the fighter of the sixties and seventies; his name was deeply enmeshed in the fabric of the Big Event. He was everything an American kid could aspire to be: rich, famous, handsome, the best in his field, sought after, trendsetter, icon, idol, good, charitable, kind, gentle, sweet, father, husband, lover, raconteur, magician, entertainer, drug-free, vice-free, individualist, revolutionary, religious leader, and, at the bottom of it all, still a mischievous kid at heart.

I'm always asked on talk shows, "Yeah, but how would he have done with Joe Louis? Or Marciano, or Dempsey?"

I try to point out gently how the sport has progressed, how the size and speed of fighters has changed. Ali, in his prime? Ali at six-foot three and 215 pounds, with the speed of a welterweight and a chin of iron, with his blurring combinations, ring generalship, and speed? That Ali?

No problem!

Dempsey was too small and too slow for Ali, and Dempsey went down. Size, speed, and ring generalship would have been the difference. If a puffed-up light heavyweight like Tunney could beat Dempsey twice, why couldn't Ali?

Joe Louis was a mechanical, by-the-book, one-two-shuffle-then-jab fighter. He was my favorite fighter, but he did have trouble with motion and cleverness. Billy Conn almost beat him, until the Irish in him took over and he decided he would *knock out* the Brown Bomber. Then, curtains. Louis never forgave a mistake.

Two legendary champions: Jack Dempsey and Ali. *Photo courtesy Hy Simon*

Conn's comments years later pretty well tell the story: "What's the use in being Irish if you can't do something dumb every once in a while."

I worked on the Ali-Marciano computer re-creation fight, and it gave me a great opportunity to see them in a ring together. Rocky was as tough as his name, but his facial tissues were as thin as Kleenex. Rocky was five-foot-nine if stretched on a rack, and he felt insulted if you missed him with a jab. "Sting like a bee" would never be more evident than in this fight. Liston, Frazier, Foreman, Shavers, Lyle, and Norton couldn't KO Ali, why would the Rock have been able to? Size and speed. Ali by TKO on cuts.

As for the rest of the greats of his time, he fought them all and beat them all. And as for the old-old-timers, take a look at the old movies. Even Jack Johnson fought in slow motion compared to Ali. No problem.

Ali's legend in the ring is well preserved for all to see; his fame, generated by media, known to all. But it is in the area of little kindnesses, of generous gestures, of anonymous gifts, that I came to appreciate Ali most of all.

His daily life was filled with the small tokens of affection. He'd stop his Rolls-Royce to shake hands with old men, play with kids on a playground, or kiss old ladies; those actions indicated a man who loved people, who loved to "shock and amaze," and who loved to entertain.

My mind flashes back to a hotel room in New York City before the first Frazier fight. Ali was watching the news. A story came on about ancient inhabitants of a Jewish nursing home who were

Winning the Thurman Award for his contribution to the Association for the Help to Retarded Children. New York City, 1990. *Photo courtesy Hy Simon*

being evicted because they couldn't come up with $100,000. It was cold in New York, and the thought of those old people on the street got to Ali. Without any discussion, he reached for the phone and called the TV station. He would donate the $100,000, provided his name not be used. Ali did not want trouble from the Muslims or from certain members of the Ali Circus who were chronically "in need." Money was given, it arrived in time, old people were saved, the curtain comes down, go to black and a happy ending.

Not quite.

Someone leaked it to the New York newspapers, and Ali was on the front page.

My favorite Ali story came to me in an unusual fashion. Ali had won his title back in Zaire, and we were returning in an Air France plane. I was seated next to an old man. Angelo brought me some newspapers, and I was busily reading our clippings and reliving the excitement of that wonderful night.

"Do you know this man?" asked the old gentleman in a tremulous voice.

"Yes. I am Ali's doctor."

"He is an unusual human being."

"Why do you say that?" I asked, intrigued that this old gentleman should have anything to do with Ali. He had already given me his colorful history. His life had been wildly adventurous. He had served in France in the Lafayette Escadrille as a fighter pilot. When the war ended, he had married a French concert pianist and stayed in France.

Late in life, they had been shocked and surprised to find the lady was pregnant. When the child reached college age, they sent him to America to obtain his education, which he did. He graduated, and his father gave him his present: He could travel to Europe on a Eurail pass, with a modest budget, but he had to be back in the United States in September in time to start on his first job, in Atlanta.

He returned to Kennedy Airport in time, but he was flat broke. With a summer beard, long hair, a backpack and combat boots, he decided to hitchhike. His chances of getting picked up in that outfit, late in the afternoon, with the sun setting, were not good.

Night was falling, along with a light, misty rain, and his chances

Ali and author in front of Miami Beach's Fontainebleau Hotel, 1976.

of making it in time to the first day of his first job were dying with the last rays of the sun.

With a screeching of tires, a limo stopped. The back door opened, and the young man jumped in and found himself facing a very attractive, albeit large, black couple.

"Where are you going on a night like this?"

The voice was unmistakable. His eyes strained to see the man's face.

Yes, no doubt about it: He had caught a ride with Muhammad Ali and his then wife, Belinda. The boy explained his predicament, and Ali laughed.

"Well, you sure ain't getting there tonight. Why don't you come home with us and we'll fix you supper and see some movies. To-morrow I'll drive you out to the expressway early so you can catch a ride."

Shocked by his good fortune, the boy tagged along, went to Ali's mansion in Cherry Hill, New Jersey, ate a huge meal, made himself a chocolate ice cream soda, and watched old cowboy films with Ali until it was time to turn in.

He woke up the next day to the smell of bacon and eggs cooking downstairs. Dressing quickly, he went down to find Ali serving up a hearty breakfast. Ali then said he'd take him to the expressway, whereupon they took off in the Rolls.

Ali drove on the expressway for a bit, then turned off at the airport and stopped at the Eastern Airline concourse. The boy looked at him in amazement.

"But I told you—I'm broke."

Ali dug into his back pocket and handed him a one-way ticket to Atlanta. He'd had one of his minions pick it up.

"It's dangerous for a college-educated boy to be out on that expressway hitchhiking."

The boy started to say something and Ali took his hand, then shook it in a firm grip.

"Pay me back when you start making some money," Ali said with his grin, and before the boy could speak, Muhammad Ali, Heavyweight Champion of the Whole Wide World, was gone.

As they used to say in the old TV series, "There are eight million stories in the Ali City," but I still think that one is my favorite.

Ali was, and is, unique. He is the perpetual child in us all, Peter Pan. His is the world of the paradox, of Alice in Wonderland. Ali is, finally and ironically, a present-day example of the calm, peaceful nonviolence of a Gandhi—and the best example of how man is made in God's image and likeness.

MUHAMMAD ALI

(Cassius Marcellus Clay, Jr.)
(The Louisville Lip)
Born, January 17, 1942, Louisville, Ky. Weight, 186–236 lbs.
Height, 6 ft. 3 in.
1959 National AAU Light Heavyweight Champion
1960 National AAU Light Heavyweight Champion
1960 Olympic Light Heavyweight Gold Medalist

1960
Oct. 29—Tunney Hunsaker, Louisville .... W   6
Dec. 27—Herb Biler, Miami Beach .... TKO   4

1961
Jan. 17—Tony Esperti, Miami Beach .... TKO   3
Feb. 7—Jim Robinson, Miami Beach .... TKO   1
Feb. 21—Donnie Fleeman, Miami Beach .... TKO   7
Apr. 19—Lamar Clark, Louisville .... KO   3
June 26—Duke Sabedong, Las Vegas .... W   10
July 22—Alonzo Johnson, Louisville .... W   10
Oct. 7—Alex Miteff, Louisville .... TKO   6
Nov. 29—Willi Bearnanoff, Louisville .... TKO   7

1962
Feb. 10—Sonny Banks, New York .... TKO   4
Feb. 28—Don Warner, Miami Beach .... TKO   4

Apr. 23—George Logan, Los Angeles .... TKO 4
May 19—Billy Daniels, New York .... TKO 7
July 20—Alejandro Lavoranta, Los Angeles .... KO 5
Nov. 15—Archie Moore, Los Angeles .... TKO 4

1963

Jan. 24—Charlie Powell, Pittsburgh .... KO 3
Mar. 13—Doug Jones, New York .... W 10
June 18—Henry Cooper, London .... TKO 5

1964

Feb. 25—Sonny Liston, Miami Beach .... TKO 7
    (Won World Heavyweight Title)

1965

May 25—Sonny Liston, Lewiston, Me. .... KO 1
    (Retained World Heavyweight Title)
July 31—Jimmy Ellis, San Juan, P.R. .... Exh. 3
July 31—Cody Jones, San Juan, P.R. .... Exh. 3
Aug. 16—Cody Jones, Gothenburg .... Exh. 2
Aug. 16—Jimmy Ellis, Gothenburg .... Exh. 2
Aug. 20—Jimmy Ellis, London .... Exh. 4
Aug. 20—Cody Jones, Paisley .... Exh. 4
Nov. 22—Floyd Patterson, Las Vegas .... TKO 12
    (Retained World Heavyweight Title)

1966

Mar. 29—George Chuvalo, Toronto .... W 15
    (Retained World Heavyweight Title)
May 21—Henry Cooper, London, Eng. .... TKO 6
    (Retained World Heavyweight Title)
Aug. 6—Brian London, London, Eng. .... KO 3
    (Retained World Heavyweight Title)
Sept. 10—Karl Mildenberger, Frankfurt .... TKO 12
    (Retained World Heavyweight Title)
Nov. 14—Cleveland Williams, Houston .... TKO 3
    (Retained World Heavyweight Title)

1967

Feb. 6—Ernest Terrell, Houston .... W 15
       (Retained World Heavyweight Title)
Mar. 22—Zora Folley, New York .... KO 7
       (Retained World Heavyweight Title)

1968–1969
(Inactive)

1970

Feb. 3—Announced retirement.
Oct. 26—Jerry Quarry, Atlanta .... TKO 3
Dec. 7—Oscar Bonavena, New York .... TKO 15

1971

Mar. 8—Joe Frazier, New York .... L 15
       (For World Heavyweight Title)
July 26—Jimmy Ellis, Houston .... TKO 12
       (Won Vacant NABF Heavyweight Title)
Nov. 17—Buster Mathis, Houston .... W 12
       (Retained NABF Heavyweight Title)
Dec. 26—Jurgen Blin, Zurich, Switz. .... KO 7

1972

Apr. 1—Mac Foster, Tokyo, Japan .... W 15
May 1—George Chuvalo, Vancouver, B.C. .... W 12
       (Retained NABF Heavyweight Title)
June 27—Jerry Quarry, Las Vegas .... TKO 7
       (Retained NABF Heavyweight Title)
July 19—Alvin (Blue) Lewis, Dublin .... TKO 11
Sept. 20—Floyd Patterson, New York .... TKO 7
       (Retained NABF Heavyweight Title)
Nov. 21—Bob Foster, Stateline, Nev. .... KO 8
       (Retained NABF Heavyweight Title)

1973

Feb. 14—Joe Bugner, Las Vegas .... W 12
Mar. 31—Ken Norton, San Diego .... L 12
       (Lost NABF Heavyweight Title)

Sept. 10—Ken Norton, Los Angeles .... W   12
        (Regained NABF Heavyweight Title)
Oct. 20—Rudi Lubbers, Jakarta .... W   12

1974

Jan. 28—Joe Frazier, New York .... W   12
        (Retained NABF Heavyweight Title)
Oct. 30—George Foreman, Kinshasa, Zaire .... KO   8
        (Regained World Heavyweight Title)

1975

Mar. 24—Chuck Wepner, Cleveland .... TKO   15
        (Retained World Heavyweight Title)
May 16—Ron Lyle, Las Vegas .... TKO   11
        (Retained World Heavyweight Title)
July   1—Joe Bugner, Kuala Lumpur .... W   15
        (Retained World Heavyweight Title)
Oct.   1—Joe Frazier, Quezon City .... TKO   14
        (Retained World Heavyweight Title)

1976

Feb. 20—Jean Pierre Coopman, San Juan, P.R. .... KO   5
        (Retained World Heavyweight Title)
Apr. 30—Jimmy Young, Landover, Md. .... W   15
        (Retained World Heavyweight Title)
May 24—Richard Dunn, Munich .... TKO   5
        (Retained World Heavyweight Title)
June 25—Antonio Inoki, Tokyo .... Exh. D   15
Sept. 28—Ken Norton, New York .... W   15
        (Retained World Heavyweight Title)

1977

May 16—Alfredo Evangelista, Landover .... W   15
        (Retained World Heavyweight Title)
Sept. 29—Earnie Shavers, New York .... W   15
        (Retained World Heavyweight Title)
Dec.   2—Scott LeDoux, Chicago, Illinois .... Exh.   5

1978

Feb. 15—Leon Spinks, Las Vegas .... L 15
    (Lost World Heavyweight Title)

Sept. 15—Leon Spinks, New Orleans .... W 15
    (Regained World Heavyweight Title)

1979

June 27—Announced retirement.

1980

Oct. 2—Larry Holmes, Las Vegas .... TKO by 11
    (For Vacant World Heavyweight Title)

1981

Dec. 11—Trevor Berbick, Nassau .... L 10

TB	KO	WD	WF	D	LD	LF	KO BY	ND	NC
61	37	19	0	0	4	0	1	0	0